Why read this book?

To learn, and do. We live on the edge of a "New Age"—not just a "time" as when the century ends or when we enter the "Aquarian Age", but an *Age*, in the same sense as used in such phrases as "The Bronze Age", "The Iron Age", "The Industrial Age", etc. It is an *Age* in the sense that Humanity is entering into a time of new technology—in fact, a new *kind* of technology that is partly *psychic*.

It isn't just the *Age* of the "Computer"—the computer is only the first, albeit important, step that is leading to the use of the *Silicon Crystal* as means to interface MAN WITH THE WORLD!

It can be called the "age of PK", for it is leading to a true extension of individual consciousness into the "outer" world with a resulting ability to manipulate energy and matter without mechanical intervention or somatic contact.

The author calls it "The New Atlantis".

Man is learning that he is *not* separate from Nature, the world we live in. Now he must accept that realization and consciously enter into that which he had mistaken for the "outer" world. And only by doing so can Man aid the natural process of purification and transformation now necessitated by the errors of pollution and abuse, thus bring us into a new Golden Age of peace and beauty.

By building the simple and inexpensive Crystal Psionic Devices, or "Psychic Power Tools" described in this book, you enter into an active role in the developing New Technology, a truly *Human* technology both dependent on and stimulating of genuine growth in consciousness.

The next evolutionary step.

Humanity *consciously* interfaced with nature.

ABOUT THE AUTHOR

Michael Gary Smith is a Piscean, born March 9, 1947 with an ancestral background that includes English, Irish, Cheyenne, German, French and Cherokee, and a conservative upbringing on a Kansas farm.

He is a past member of the Bear Tribe Medicine Society and a psychic healer, and today works for a Silicon Valley electronics company.

"My great grandfather (a Colorado Cheyenne medicine man) didn't distinguish between red and white men because he knew, as the prophecies of his people said, of a time when red brothers, white brothers, yellow brothers and black brothers would start to recognize each other as such. He knew the planetary influences on the part of the Earth Mother we know as North America would gradually influence the humans living on it to evolve into what he called "real people", which could be recognized by the balance of the Star Father and Earth Mother apparent in their minds and hearts—inside, not outside."

It is perhaps the traditional Piscean characteristic of psychic sensitivity (he has Mercury conjunct Sun in Pisces) that led him into the "inner" world of Nature and the Crystal to give us this unique vision of a new "race" of Real People, of a new Psychic Technology, and a new ethic of Star born Warriors.

To Write to the Author

We cannot guarantee that every letter written to the author can be answered, but all will be forwarded on to him. Both the author and the publisher appreciate hearing from readers and learning of your enjoyment and benefit from this book. Llewellyn also publishes *The New Times*, a bi-monthly news magazine of New Age esoteric studies, and some readers' questions and comments may be answered through the *New Times'* columns if permission to do so is included in your letter. The author does participate in seminars and workshops, and dates and places may be announced in *The Llewellyn New Times*. To write to the author, or to secure a free sample copy of the *New Times*, write to:

Michael G. Smith
c/o THE LLEWELLYN NEW TIMES
P.O. Box 64383-Dept. 725, St. Paul, MN 55164-0383 U.S.A.

Please enclose a self-addressed, stamped envelope for reply, or $1.00 to cover expenses.

ABOUT LLEWELLYN'S PSI-TECH SERIES

The *Psyche* — we really don't know much about it.

But we do know that it has amazing powers, and that we are witness to these powers in Psychic Phenomena, Radionics and Psionics, in Prophecy, in Divination and Dowsing, in Healing, and in miracles and mysteries of all kinds.

Over the whole history of humanity, these powers have been experienced and cultivated by Shamans, Magicians, Witches, Holy (whole) Men and Women, and people-in-need.

There are many *technologies* for developing and applying these little known powers. Even when we lack understanding of how something works, we can still see that it does work, at least sometimes, and find ways to apply it to our own benefit. We do this all the time. How many people "know" how electricity works? How does the body heal itself? How does love join more than bodies? What kind of world would we have if we couldn't benefit from these?

The *Psyche* — it is part of us, and yet is separable from the body; it is "personal", yet it connects us to the whole world we live in; it makes us aware of things, yet mostly continues beyond our awareness; it gives us life, yet continues on beyond death. It is soul and spirit together; it is mind and emotion and our Higher Self; it is the "beast" within *and* the "god and goddess" within.

In Llewellyn's PSI-TECH Series of books and tapes, we focus on *techniques* for tapping these many powers of the Psyche, including those that join Psyche and Body, Man and Earth, Life and Cosmos in the many ways we perceive yet do not understand.

Within this series we do not include subjects that are highly "codified" where the applications have been reduced to well-established rules (as in Astrology or Magical Ritual) or where the procedures for study are primarily those of the physical sciences (as with much of parapsychology). Rather we interest ourselves in subjects where we perceive the phenomena and can apply aspects of it to our benefit, but the how and why remain mostly filled with mystery.

With this series, we hope to contribute to the process by which these New Frontiers become better understood, and their applications more practical and available to the benefit of everyone.

CRYSTAL POWER

by Michael G. Smith

1986
Llewellyn Publications
St. Paul, Minnesota, 55164-0383, U.S.A.

International Standard Book Number: 0-87542-725-1
Library of Congress Catalog Number: 84-48089

First Edition, 1985
First Printing, 1985
Second Printing, 1985
Third Printing, 1985
Fourth Printing, 1986
Fifth Printing, 1986

Cover Art: Steve Fastner

Produced by Llewellyn Publications
Typography and Art property of Chester-Kent, Inc.

Published by
LLEWELLYN PUBLICATIONS
A Division of Chester-Kent, Inc.
P.O. Box 64383
St. Paul, MN 55164-0383, U.S.A.
Printed in the United States of America

This book is dedicated to the strength, understanding, intelligence, creativity, endurance, honesty, and spirit of middle class working people everywhere.

My appreciation and thanks to Diane Simmons and Pat Bayhouse for their assistance and support and Todd Jackson for his superb graphics.

CONTENTS

INTRODUCTION: TOOLS OF CHANGE

THIS BOOK IS DIFFERENT. You've probably opened many books expecting to find everything from the mysteries of the Ancients and the Universe to the future secrets of advanced science. Usually there's only a written philosophy that sounds wonderful, but you have seen it before. You won't find that in this book. Like me, you may have found marvelous teasing descriptions of incredible inventions used by ancient civilizations and you were probably frustrated by the lack of any explanation of how these devices worked or how people used them. Any design or instructions on how to build them were conspicuous by their absence.

Someone else certainly did build and use some advanced equipment, but it was always thousands of years ago and usually on the other side of the world or, worse, somewhere else in space . . . about 400 light years away is the standard description.

The other place you've read of fantastic machines is in futurist science stories. In most cases, too often, you realized you were going to be long gone before you ever saw one of these. Besides that, only a select group of scientists knew about them and it took millions of dollars to build them. Like many of us, you may have thought, "I wish I could learn how those work, or how to build one, or just plain get my hands on one . . . live and in person . . . right now!"

That's what this book is for, and that's why it's so different. It tells you how to construct the things that people like you and I have dreamed of for so long. Not only that, most of them are simple and inexpensive to build. They're normally more economical than many hobbies. You'll probably be pleasantly surprised.

If you're interested in ancient science, space science, or super science of the future, this book is for you. It's here for YOU, not somewhere else in someone else's hands. It's HERE NOW, not in the ancient past or in the far future. IT IS HERE FOR YOU NOW!

Ancient priests and priestesses have been described as working with remarkable tools which produced miracles, even by today's standards. The staff of Moses is thought to have been handed down from the time of Atlantis. The ancient scientist cutting stones and levitating them into place has become a routine description. The holy man in robes, effecting miraculous healings with a magic wand, is a tradition. The hooded wizard, appearing out of thin air with staff in hand, is a standard fantasy. The American Indian Medicine Man with a bag containing a magic crystal was common many years ago. The Eastern mystic who used a crystal to produce clouds and rain is also talked about quite frequently.

Could it be that at one time these were not merely symbols of power? Is it possible that they once were really the *tools* of power? Do the myths still carry truth after thousands of years of telling?

If there is any truth at all in these myths, it should be possible to duplicate the advanced science of the Ancients. It is reasonable to expect to find it compatible with modern science, particularly in the areas of particle and field physics.

Two decades ago, I didn't think it was possible to find the facts and separate them from the myths. If any of these wild stories turned out to be true, it would surpass the most outrageous science fiction or fantasy ever written. I wanted to know enough to understand that either this was an example of people's daydreams or that a small percentage was fact and could be reproduced by people like you and me.

Almost everyone who deals with ancient knowledge or occult secrets is willing to talk about it—they talk about it too much, actually. I didn't believe any of this hocus-pocus could be real, so I started asking some hard, specific questions. I decided to call their bluff. Most of the time, that's exactly what it turned out to be.

When someone was telling me their story about a previous life as an Atlantean priest, I would ask them, "If you were there, describe the tools you used. Tell me exactly what your rod of power looked like. What kind of materials was it made out of? How long was the staff you used? What kind of stone was in your headband or crown? What was it used for? How many other people used these? Were they used by men and/or women? Most important, how was it built? How did it work? What part of this advanced science did you deal with? Healing? Weapons? Energy? Transportation? What? I want to know and I want to know right now!"

Needless to say, many people found my questions disconcerting. I didn't make many friends by asking hard questions about people's most cherished inner beliefs. I did gain concrete information about a great many things that technically could not exist, but apparently did exist. Although these were not clear, complete answers, there were enough of them from so many different sources that the patterns of truth were starting to appear.

Just this part of the experiment took over ten years, but persistence pays off in any field. After a decade, I finally had enough information to reconstruct the first piece of equipment. This was the Atlantean Power Rod, also known as the Rod and Staff of Moses, or Energy Rod. Understanding how it worked or what it did, or even exactly what it really was came years later.

At first, building the long sought-after artifact was quite enough to prove to me that there was some basic truth to the legends of the past after all. This meant a lot more to me than visualizing white light or meditating on something-or-other. Here at last was a machine that could be built, studied, held and experimented with. Now, I have no proof that Atlantis or any comparable civilization ever existed in the past. All I have is the fact that devices of a sophisticated technology are here today and will be more abundant in the future.

Among the creations that have been rebuilt are such things as the psi headband, the large quartz crystal/copper disc communicator, the force knife and sword, the personal energy shield, the home and garden force field generator, over half a dozen types of power rods and staffs, the crystal pendulum device, the crystal contrivance said to be used by prophets, interdimensional doors, and assorted tools for healers and warriors. These are not just vague references, but diagrams and instructions you can use to build them. They can be built by anyone, and they can be built economically, as well.

I can't be responsible for how these are built and used, since that varies as much as different people do. However, I am sure that you will find them interesting and exciting. You'll find things that have not been in any other book you've read before. That's the exciting part. I hope you enjoy it.

Michael G. Smith
January 1983

PROLOGUE

"THE WINDS OF FIRE SWEEP THE PLAINS OF TIME"

Imagine a scene, thousands of years ago, in a civilization with a higher state of development that we have now. Amid the shining white marble pillars, an old, gray-haired man in a blue robe walks through an arched doorway. Once inside the courtyard, he sits near a sparkling fountain, centered in a garden and surrounded by lush plants. As the sick and ailing people start to arrive, he takes a rod out of the sleeve of his robe. His piercing eyes glance upward as he raises his arm, pointing the rod toward the sun. The rays of the sun explode into the colors of the rainbow as they pass through the quartz crystal at the top end of the rod, and the cap at the bottom shines with a copper/gold hue.

A young boy approaches timidly, cradling an obviously broken arm against his body. The healer places one hand gently under the boy's arm as he points the sharp-pointed crystal portion of the rod at the injured part. An electric sensation fills the air as invisible energy flows from the rod into the boy's arm. The broken bone knits together immediately. The same natural healing process that would normally take weeks has been done in a matter of seconds.

The old man in the blue robe takes no payment. The grateful smile on the little boy's face is reward enough. Again, the rod is aimed at the blind eyes of an old woman. The expression on her face as she sees for the first time in many years brings a smile of kindness to the healer. On it goes, all day long.

Three thousand years later, near an ancient city on a high plateau in the mountains of South America, a young warrior steps out into the morning sun. Across the field stands his adversary, also a young warrior. Both young men wear the red-feathered battle dress. Each man pulls an Energy Rod from his belt, pointing it at his enemy. A shield around each warrior glows blue/white hot as the energies of the Power Rods attempt to penetrate defenses. The personal body shields are produced by the same energy that comes through the war rods.

At the same instant, they realize it's a stalemate and swing the rods in a clockwise motion at the sky. In less than a moment, black clouds form above and lightning bolts strike, burning and blackening the ground around each of them. A draw again until one combatant drops flat to the ground aiming his rod at the enemy with both hands. A second later a hurricane-like wind sweeps the battlefield; the second warrior is blown away and killed, dashed against the rocks strewn about the area.

The victor returns to his city, satisfied that the territorial dispute has been settled with the death of only one chosen soldier. The innocent men, women, and children of his tribe are safe and well as the losing chief surrenders his territory to the victorious chief.

A civilized war, if such can ever be, is over. Perhaps in our time we could learn this lesson.

Many years have now passed and an old holy man is leading his people away from danger in the Middle East. As he approaches the Red Sea, he raises his staff to the sky. The energy with which the crystal tip is charged is released. The sea parts in two, making a path for his people to escape the quickly approaching soldiers. When the people have safely crossed the sea, he turns to watch the troops enter the path. Raising the crystal staff again, Moses points at the walls of water and the force field vanishes immediately. The walls of water rush together to drown the enemy.

The information you are about to see is for people like you and me who have an intense desire to be on the frontier, the sharp edge of change, in hope of a better world. Creating a new world or recreating an ancient one is not the way to security, but it is the way to an exciting, interesting and purposeful life.

It may be important to mention that besides describing how to construct various psionic and subatomic particle devices, we will attempt to anticipate the possible effects of these devices on our present-day society and recall the influence of these machines on societies throughout history. We will also attempt to point out the responsibilities of individuals involved in using New Age technology. This is a radical departure from the general practice of our time, which is to invent something and mass-produce it as fast as possible, giving no thought to the long-term effects of any product whether it is an automobile or a nuclear bomb.

The process described in this book is designed to stimulate thinking and growth. We will be pointing out the positive effects of reintroducing this knowledge into our society, and the negative effects that can result as well.

One point to consider is that we are describing an alien technology—or one that is quite different from the thinking processes most of us have been taught. We are also describing science and knowledge that borders on the edge of mysticism on one hand, and particle physics on the other. In both of these areas of study, our language has proven to be a limiting factor which can only be used to represent or approximate the concepts and techniques involved.

The reintroduction of this type of knowledge into our society is a process that has been progressing rapidly in recent years, although it began a long time ago. This book is part of that process. It is a part that requires the use of intuitive perception. This is necessary to understand the limited language's symbolic representation of concepts that reflect the subatomic universe in relation to the chaotic times we live in.

I've spent half of my life learning enough to share this with you. If you want, you can take it from here. It is probably the most difficult endeavor you could undertake. It may turn out to be the most fulfilling opportunity of this age.

The psionic subatomic particle machines outlined in this book promote individual growth and expanded consciousness. The book itself describes a variety of experiences that should promote and stimulate growth and awareness. It is with hope that I make this knowledge available to anyone who wants it when such knowledge has previously been hidden and hoarded.

Responsibility and creativity are the main ingredients involved. This is the stuff that dreams are made of—good dreams, not the other kind. With much love, light, and balance, I cheerfully welcome you to the thought of the subatomic age.

TOOLS OF CHANGE

Psionic Devices of Quartz Crystal

CHAPTER ONE

PAST NOW—FUTURE NOW

*"Power? You know nothing of real power if you
pretend it is dependent on fame, wealth, and the
approval of other people. Go stand alone on the
mountain. If your personal power is exactly the
same as it was before, you have the power. That is
the true essence of power."*

The Atlantean Power Rods were brought to the Planet
Earth long before the time of Atlantis. Although the people
who used them may have come here over 400 million years
ago, we'll look at a time nearly 80,000 years in the past.
Even at the peak of this civilization, only a few priests,
kings, doctors, and soldiers had access to the Rods and
Staffs of power. These people were capable of projecting
the universal force of creative energies into the so-called
physical dimension. Though they were far more advanced
mentally than our present society, these people still did
not evolve beyond arrogant personal power games. The
destruction that resulted from the abuse in that age is so
far lost in the past that it is only spoken of today as an
ancient myth, the lost continent preceding the Days of
Atlantis. In fact, it is so far removed from us that it is
useless to even speak of it today.

Atlantis may be closer to us, but not by much. At the
peak of Atlantean civilization, perhaps 10,000 to 15,000
years ago the ruling classes, who were the only ones having

these high energy power tools, achieved great works in the fields of architecture, medicine, art, communication and climate control, and had energy to bring about a very high standard of living. Being all too human, however, they also achieved a very high standard of efficiency in the practice of war. They were much better at it then we are today, if "better" is the proper term to use.

Few, if any, traces remain to mark the mistakes of this so-called great civilization. There are signs that some of the carriers of knowledge escaped the destruction of their homeland. The traces are still in evidence in Asia, South America, Europe, Africa and North America. Even in the comparatively recent Bible, there are references to the ancient power tools of the priesthood. The most widely known are those of Moses and Aaron. What, exactly were these Rods and Staffs of Moses and Aaron?

Power Rods and Staffs were used by Moses and Aaron, although the descriptions in the Bible are only of the *effects* of these devices, not the devices themselves. *Exodus* has many vivid descriptions of the dramatic results of super-technology, such as the one in Chapter 9:23, 24:

> "And Moses lifted up his staff toward heaven; and the Lord sent thunder and hail, and lightning ran along the ground; and the Lord showered hail upon the land of Egypt."

> "So there was hail, and flaming fire mingled with hail, very grievous, such as had never been in all the land of Egypt since it became a nation."

No wonder Moses said, "Thy rod and thy staff, they comfort me". He stood alone against the armies of the Pharaoh. Not only that, he won. What kind of rod and staff did he have? Powerful, no doubt!

The Atlantean history of these rods and staffs cannot be verified. The descriptions in the Bible did come, however indirectly, from someone who had seen them. What are these machines of magic doing here now? When did they reappear?

To the best of my knowledge, they were recreated in 1975 in the United States. The first one was constructed in the state of Washington. By 1977, information on the building and basic use of these devices was available to a limited number of people in the Northwest.

The response to public seminars and workshops on constructing and operating Power Rods was overwhelming. Many people who saw them or held one for the first time seemed to feel familiar with them instantly. There was a magnetic attraction to these devices. There was also a demand for more and more information about them.

What kind of people were interested in these esoteric artifacts? At first, it appeared that only occultists, seekers of hidden knowledge, and spiritual devotees were attracted. However, soon it became noticeable that people who normally had no contact with this type of information were extremely interested. Everybody seemed excited by it. There were electronics engineers, grandmothers, construction workers, salespeople, students (both teenage and younger), school teachers, geologists and, in general, a complete cross-section of America. People of all age groups, vocations, men and women, and, of course, the usual number of people that deal with secret knowledge as a routine (psychics, ministers, astrologers, healers, medicine people) and a few all-out weirdos.

What did some of these people do with the information they received about building and using Power Rods and Staffs? In the last few years, they apparently have been doing anything they can think of. The experiments have been many and as varied as you can imagine. The claims have been outrageous to say the least. Some people have said that they achieved fantastic effects in healings of both humans and animals. Charging and increasing the growth of plants has been a very popular use. A common entertainment has been the influencing of compass needles.

Further claims have included influencing all types of electronic instruments from computers to traffic lights.

Some have said that magnetometers showed a reading of the beams and fields emitted from the Rods. Others claimed distance made no difference. Effects were noted at five feet as well as a thousand miles. Later, we'll explain why this could be so.

Regardless of the claims for uses of Power Rods and Staffs, these devices are widely in use in our society today. How widely? In the United States in about 35 states, as well as in Canada, Australia, New Zealand, Great Britain and the Netherlands. What's so unusual about their widespread use is that they've never been widely advertised. From the mid-70s on, the knowledge has been passed from friend to friend, both in written forms and by word of mouth. Word travels fast when the subject is as exciting as this.

What does this mean for you and me? That is for you to decide after you have seen what is now known about the machines of the Ancients.

No matter what the fantastic visions of the ancient past or the super space-age dreams of the future, one thing is clear. This information is available for you to experiment with right now. In the following chapters, we'll explore it as completely as we can.

Are you ready to deal with such things as matter being created by thought? An electron that travels backward in time only to be transformed into a positron? Events and prophecies of the ages that turn out to be effects that took place in time BEFORE the causes occurred? Try to think of particles that travel at the speed of light or faster; it gets more complex: some of them appear in two places in space and time simultaneously.

Even Einstein had a struggle working with this, but you don't have to be a mathematician to grasp what's going on in your world, in your Universe. The average person may use only three to five percent of his or her mind. Exceptional individuals may use ten percent of their total capabilities. Einstein is said to have used thirteen to fifteen percent of his total mental capacity. Even that isn't much.

We can probably do better.

Try using twenty percent or more of your thinking and feeling talents. We won't even deal with trying to use anything near fifty or one hundred percent. That's awe-inspiring to even think of. Using high energy power tools like these usually pushes people far beyond their normal self-imposed limits. That's quite enough for now.

We live in the most interesting and exciting times that have ever existed on this planet. What's more, we are creating and recreating them ourselves. It's a fun responsibility, growing more so every day. Are you ready? Ready or not, now is the time!

Thinking In — Thinking Out

What you think is what you get. You're probably familiar with most of the positive thinking procedures and how they apply to your life. They always work. The only difference is how fast or how slowly they work. In this case, the main priority is cutting down the time, making it work faster.

That's the name of the game. It's a *time game*. Your time is important. You're aware that thoughts, both positive and negative, are amplified by emotions (feelings and desires). There are machines that work on exactly that basis. They were created for people who can grasp the simplicity of the process.

"Simple" does not always mean *easy*. It becomes easy like anything else, after you've done it a few times. The first time doesn't seem quite so easy. Like a computer, what you feed in is exactly what you get out. Except in this case, it's amplified, increased ten times; one hundred times; one thousand times; or even ten thousand times.

You are in control of the total process; no one else is. That probably sounds intriguing because there are usually very few things we feel in control of during these times of transition. Consider the economy. Of course we really do "control" it in conjunction with the 4 billion or so other people within the mass mind. That's chaos, all right.

In the case of Energy Rods, the individual is the only control; the operator is totally responsible for the results or lack of results. If you've thought you were a reincarnated priest/priestess from the lost continent of Atlantis, you are in luck. If you are a modern day wizard, sorcerer/sorceress, have at it. If you've fantasized about being a magician with a magic wand, here's your chance. If you are a scientist/researcher striving to unlock the secrets of the Universe, relativity, space and time, you are now closer than you think.

Whatever you think you want in this lifetime, right now, go for it. The tools of change are yours for the asking and/or using. There is no one to stop you or stand in your way but yourself.

Healers and Warriors

These are the tools of healers and warriors. It may sound like a contradiction or an unlikely combination, but greatest healers are often also the most powerful warriors. The difference is a matter of polarity because the super science for both is based on the same forces of the Universe. The common denominator, whether considered as all one energy or as varying states of matter, is still an understanding of the process of creation/destruction. Positive or negative, the energy is action flows the same regardless of the end result.

Good or bad is a question of personal opinion and judgment. The actions of the healer can be based on positive or negative energy equally. If a broken bone needs mending, the flow of universal energy is definitely of a positive nature. However, if the problem is a destructive virus or germ infection, the flow of universal energy is of a negative nature, since it is intended to destroy the organism causing the disease.

In the way of the warrior, the energy can easily be either positive or negative. A soldier, armed with a War Rod, will try to disrupt the flow of the life force of the enemy, a definitely negative action. However, the reason can well be to prevent the enemy from oppressing the warrior's own people, a positive action.

In expressing life and growth, the healer and warrior are one and the same. Both the healer and the warrior embody the forces of creation and of destruction at the same time. With the understanding and operation of Power Rods and Staffs, the individual becomes responsible for the uses to which their power is directed, whether for good or evil.

"Power" is an expression we should explore in a little more detail. The concept of personal, individual power is of particular interest to us here. In our present time, power is associated with the acquisition of billions of dollars, a business empire, or even the tax money empire of the government. This is merely an artificial myth. The achievement of fame as a means to power is a myth in its own way also. "Power" achieved through wealth and/or fame is artificial because it depends upon other people to feed it.

Look back into the ancient past at the Atlantean priest/scientist. A priest or priestess of that time could, and often did, separate personal power from the people. Standing high on a mountain top in a new land, they had just as much personal power as they possessed in a rich city surrounded by people. Even today, Native American medicine men and women laugh at what white culture commonly calls power. They know that all alone in the wilderness, the power they carry is just as strong, and more often stronger, than when they are surrounded by their followers.

Knowledge and understanding bring power that is not dependent on an outside source. These are the keys to true power and are inside most of us. People in our society generally use only a small amount of their potential. Ninety percent is still to be realized and used. This is where the true energy crisis is to be found; it is in human mental energy that the crisis exists.

This situation is of our own making, or the lack of our making. Americans are a handheld, machine-oriented people. We need some type of gizmo to hold in our hands as a symbol of action. The boom in pocket calculators, home computers, and video games is evidence of this. Now there is nothing wrong with this at all. The question becomes: do we dare, as individuals, hold subatomic particle beam and field generators using the creative forces of the Universe? This is the foundation of growth and development that we've built for ourselves. Do we stand up and take responsibility for it?

One of the most valuable uses for Energy Rods is in the area of healing. An Energy Rod uses the same life force (God force) that motivates the human body, the same life force of the Universe that flows through all space, time, and matter. The energy of Power Rods is really nothing new to most people, although the use of intense amounts of this energy combined with an accurate focus through a tool is a technique not widely known yet.

In the process of healing, the energy from the rod is used to remove energy blockages in the biomagnetic field of the body. This provides a balanced flow of the body's life-force energy. Removing the energy blocks provides a balance, while the body actually does the healing itself. This type of healing is easily done with plants, animals, and people.

Anyone can learn to construct a Universal Energy Rod in a relatively short time. The energy used is natural and basic to life; the technique of operation is simple. In many societies, children as young as eight years old were taught to use Energy Rods. It was considered routine for a mother to be able to heal her own children when they were injured or ill.

At one time, household pets and farm animals were healed by most members of the family who had learned of this natural process. It was considered reasonable for everyone to have some degree of skill in the area of medicine and healing. With simply-operated, high-energy tools, this was easily possible. It was possible in the past, and it is possible now. It is a part of ancient tradition that powerful healing tools of this type were used throughout history. It is predictable that these high energy devices will be used again in the future, as we grow wiser. What has not been widely known is the fact that this type of energy equipment is available and already in use by people like you and me, right now, today. It can be built by anyone, using common materials, and at a low cost in both time and money.

In the near future, the need for personal Energy Rods may become more evident. It will be necessary for individuals to be able to take direct and prompt action in solving their problems. It may not be possible for people to avoid the personal responsibility for self-healing in the near future. Many people have found it necessary to take constructive action already. After all, we're breathing poisonous gas for air, drinking impure water, and eating contaminated food as a result of our present society. A majority of the people are grievously suffering from severe mental emotional, spiritual, and physical disorders and diseases. This is even more disturbing when we realize that most of the diseases or disorders are from a social order and environment that we, ourselves, have created, are still creating, and are personally responsible for.

In the area of health and healing, all diseases become curable. The use of Universal Energy Rods is actually a simple process that allows the equal balance of the body to be restored. The affected organism heals itself. This solves what we now consider some very serious problems, both in health and economics.

The civilizing effects of the widespread use of universal energy on the society in which it is applied can be far-reaching and beneficial. Whenever individuals begin using Power Rods and Staffs, the Law of One becomes quickly manifested. The reasonable pattern is that societies held together by negative thoughts and emotions such as selfishness, greed, fear, anger, envy, jealousy, etc., break down into smaller tribal groups or communities. If the problem of war on a large scale becomes resolved the civilizing effects begin; crime, disease, and poverty soon begin to disappear.

That's the reasonable pattern. The other side of the polarity is mass destruction as a result of war for the usual stupid reasons of greed, fear, incompetence, and insecurity. I've heard many tales saying that the wrong choice was made in times long past. We are at a critical point in our development where a hard choice must be made, or else.

It's common to call our age the Nuclear Age or the Age of Aquarius. More appropriate terms may be the Crystal Age, the New Atlantean Age, the Space Age, or the Subatomic Age. As I've said before, there may be no proof that Atlantis ever existed in the past. There are signs, however, that it is here now and will be with us into the future.

One of the main characteristics of this age is the use of crystals for the manipulation of invisible energy. This is widespread throughout our world. Crystals are now an integral part of our lifestyle. They serve us in many areas and influence us in quite a few others. Many types of radios use crystals. Radio communication around the Earth and into space is a routine feature of our everyday world. The magic of television by satellite to all parts of the world is taken for granted by most people.

Liquid crystal displays appear everywhere from computers to wristwatches; microwave ovens to washing machines; calculators to sewing machines; video games to advertising signs; and the list goes on forever with new applications being developed continuously. Our transportation, from aircraft to spacecraft, from ships to automobiles, looks more like traveling electronic labs than anything else. The crystals and the liquid crystal display screens are usually doing one major task, monitoring and regulating the invisable energy that runs our society.

The undercurrent behind the scenes is always moving. The forces surround us and pass through us at all times. Some are man-controlled, others naturally produced from Earth and even deep space. The invisible energy of electricity is now the foundation of our civilization. Electrons moving along the wires of our lives affect every aspect of them. Each set of wires from home and business to power station to satellite TV is sending out interacting electromagnetic fields with their constant streams of energy radiation.

We virtually live and move and have our being in electromagnetic radiation fields. Artificial or natural, it runs around and through us in billions of particles every second and minute, of the days of our lives. It is the very fact of our existence. We'd do well to understand it as much as we can.

There is usually, but not always, a distinction between manmade artificial radiation and natural radiation. In the forms we contact every day, the man-made energy usually comes from high voltage fields and sources. The natural background radiation from Earth and from space is usually of a low voltage nature. Somehow, we imagine that higher voltage, more, is better. Is it really? What does the low voltage energy do? It does virtually everything. The low voltage generator we call Earth runs all the plants, animals, people, and all the other life-forms on the entire plant. It runs the water system, weather, earth movements, and all of the Earth's own activities combined. That's a lot. Not only that, it works extremely efficiently and constantly, unfailingly.

The biomagnetic field forces of our bodies feed off of the Earth's magnetic field and interacting interstellar fields at the same time. This provides for movement, self-healing, thought, temperature, all of the vital signs we express. It is a remarkable self-governing system and it's all running on low voltage.

The trend of the future is to duplicate nature's super-sophisticated low voltage energy systems and apply them to man's environmental lifestyle. Not only is it more economical, it works better. It has been thoroughly tested in the most advanced laboratory in existence, the Universe.

One of the most common minerals on Earth is a key to this super-science. Quartz, silicon dioxide, SiO_2, in its clear-tipped crystal form, has the natural characteristics necessary for tremendous creative uses by anyone inclined to use it. Quartz is common, cheap, and readily available in most rock shops. In the next section, we'll take a closer look at the possibilities of quartz crystals.

CHAPTER TWO

QUARTZ CRYSTAL ENERGY RODS AND STAFFS

"Civilization? We don't have a civilization now. We have a society of barbarians with a moderate degree of technology. We do have the basic foundation to develop a society of civilized people that will lead to a real civilization someday."

What is it and what does it look like? The Atlantean Power Rod is a very simple device, physically. Mentally and emotionally, it is the essence of the ancient super-science.

The basic rod is a hollow copper tube with a copper cap at one end, and approximately ¾" to 1" in diameter. At the other end is a quartz crystal. The quartz crystal (silicon dioxide, Sio_2) is also about ¾" to 1" in diameter. It is approximately 1½" to 3" long. The tip of the crystal should have clear, unchipped facets (the six-sided point of quartz). The outer covering (insulation) is leather, wrapped in a spiral (flat-wrapped is okay). For the leather insulation wrapping, black is a good color for a Combat Rod; blue, green, or even red are good colors for Healing Rods.

Some Healing Rods have quartz crystals in both ends and some have just one crystal with a copper end cap at the other end. The staffs are the same dimensions, except the main copper tube is about 5 feet long. This copper tube acts as an energy accumulator, or funnel, the leather is an insulator, and the quartz crystal acts as an energy transducer, capacitor, and focus for the beam of energy (subatomic) particles). This will be explained in further detail later.

A key learning process for achieving a workable understanding of these devices is to build your own. The moment you pick up your rod and hold it in your hand, you'll feel something different. This may be a tingling sensation of energy or a feeling of familiarity and kinship, as if you've held one before. In another life-time, or in a vision/dream, you may have. There's really no adequate way to describe it until it's been experienced personally. The experience is well worth the small amount of work and money required.

With no moving parts, the only thing that moves through an Energy Rod is energy. Unlike the machines we are more familiar with, it does not malfunction or break down. It operates in the exact degree of power and efficiency as the operator it is attuned to. As soon as construction is complete, it begins functioning in the passive mode, radiating energy in all directions from the crystal. Picked up by the individual, it continues to operate in the same manner. When the operator focuses it by pointing and thinking/visualizing, a blue-white ray of energy beams in that direction from the point of the quartz crystal at the end. Thought switches the device from passive radiating energy to an active energy beam. Intensity and distance of the beam are determined by a combination of thoughts amplified by the emotions of the individual operator.

At first, these concepts may appear to be alien to us. For many people, they immediately seem familiar and comfortable. These concepts and procedures are in harmony and balance with that inner teachings of most major religious philosophies. They also compare favorably with the principles of positive thinking and visualization involved in many of the present-day self-improvement courses. It's basic and simple—what the individual operator thinks and feels become the results. Although universal in scope and action, energy-wise the responsibility is definitely a personal one.

Universal Energy Rods and Staffs do meet certain requirements. The energy used in a positive mode in these tools is basic and harmonious to all life forms. It is also the basic creative force of the Universe in which we live. The supply of energy is unlimited and available 24 hours a day, every day. It is independent of economic, political, or even religious influence. The materials for constructing these tools are common and of so low a cost as to be readily accessible to any person who desires to build and use them. These tools are advanced and sophisticated, rather than complex, and require little or no maintenance or repairs over a long period of use. The side effects of the energy fields of these devices are not only harmless, but are actually beneficial to life, growth, and health. (We'll look at negative polarity in detail, later.)

These machines are capable of delivering a large amount of accurately focused energy at short or long distances with little or no time delay involved. The operator does not have to move or travel to affect its usage. These tools, in the hands of an experienced operator, have the theorectical ability to reach out through space and time, transforming both energy and matter on a subatomic level. Transforming radioactive substances into harmless elements is now well within the realm of possibility, as is the transformation of other harmful substances like poison chemicals, dirty air, contaminated food and water, even the Earth itself. These transmutations are completely natural processes. The Earth will disperse, transform, and purify itself over a long period of time. These devices merely speed up already normal processes.

The biblical description of Jesus transforming water into wine was a perfectly natural process. After all, nature does this all the time. The rain falls on the seeds which grow into grapevines. The grapes are picked and the fermentation process, a normal decay of matter, begins. The only difference is that the process is speeded up by the direct conversion of particles of water into wine on a subatomic level.

If you want to see how similar most elements are, look at the atomic table of elements in a science book. There's usually only a few particles of difference between the elements. It's just a matter of structure by arrangement of subatomic particles. Of course, the process of change does sometimes take place beyond space and time as we usually think of them.

The relationship of these tools to the individual is of a nature that promotes the growth of awareness/consciousness, the individual's physical, emotional, mental, and spiritual abilities and talents. Many people who grow in experience and understanding of Universal Energy Tools find they are capable of using energy for healing and balancing without using the tools. That's the sure sign of a good tool. With steady progress, the operator becomes less, instead of more, dependent on this technology. That's quite a change from the present dominant technology in our society.

These tools are such that an operator will find that they are functional in other dimensions, planes, and on other planets in the Universe, if this becomes necessary or desirable. The experience and understanding derived from the construction and use of Universal Energy Equipment is such that if the operator does not continue to maintain a physical body, he or she will still be able to function according to his or her understanding of the creative energy of this Universe gained through experience with these tools.

Many people feel an intuitive familiarity with these Energy Rods and Staffs. It may be from a previous incarnation in one of the ancient civilizations of Earth, or even another lifetime on another planet. It may be from references in ancient writings, or even present day UFO reports. Whatever the reason, it's scientifically logical from an engineer's standpoint. Many engineers and researchers agree that as advances in sophistication are made, machines become simpler instead of more complex. This is the case in mind/particle machines. They are in balance with universal laws and physics, being both sensible and practical. The fundamental application is balance and healing, whether applied to people, plants, animals, poisoned air, polluted food, contaminated water, or our chemically and radio-actively suffering Earth Mother. Total overall balance and healing is a top priority to many of us in this lifetime.

I suggest that you start with an Energy Rod for your beginning project. You can easily build a Staff later on. We'll now discuss the basic tools and materials necessary, where to acquire them, and a step-by-step construction procedure.

Only a few small hand tools are needed:

A hacksaw or tubing cutter (for cutting the copper tube)

A pair of pliers (for bending the end of the tube to fit the crystal)

A tube of instant bonding glue (for gluing the crystal and leather to the tube)

A pair of scissors (for cutting the leather insulation)

A pocket or razor knife (for trimming and scraping)

Materials needed for building the Atlantean Power Rod:

12" copper pipe, ¾" in diameter (available from most hardware stores)

¾" copper cap for one end

Leather strip ½" wide, 3' in length (any color will do)

Quartz crystal, ¾" to 1" in diameter, 2" to 3" in length (available at most rock shops). The crystal should have as clear a tip as possible, with un-chipped facets.

With the materials and tools acquired, we're ready to construct our first Energy Rod. The basic steps for building are:

1. If the copper tube isn't precut to 12" in length, use your hacksaw to cut it.
2. Put the copper cap on one end of the tube to make sure it fits easily; remove the cap and put a few drops of glue around the inside. Place the

cap back on the copper tube and press it down as far as it will go. Do this quickly; this glue dries fast.

3. Prepare the tube for mounting the crystal by cutting four slots in it lengthwise. One cut with the hacksaw makes two slots at a time, about 2½" long. Slots are cut lengthwise at the end for the crystal.

4. With slots cut, there are four sections that can be bent outward for the crystal to slide into the tube with only an inch of clear tip protruding.

5. After you use the pliers to bend the slotted tube end to fit the crystal, glue the crystal to the sides of the tube. Small strips of leather can be inserted into the spaces between the inside of the tube and the crystal with glue to make a tight seal.

6. When the crystal and the end cap are securely attached to the tube, the long strip of leather can be wrapped in a spiral and glued as it's wrapped. Put a drop of glue on the tube with every wrap and pull the leather tight until the glue dries, usually about 30 seconds to 1 minute. Don't get the glue on your fingers or the outside area of the wrap where it will show. It won't take much glue for a tight, permanent fit.

7. After the glue on the leather is dry and tight, use the knife to trim the leather edges around the copper end cap and the quartz crystal.

You have just finished building your first Energy Rod.

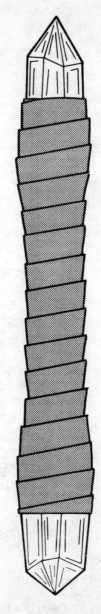

DOUBLE CRYSTAL HEALING ROD

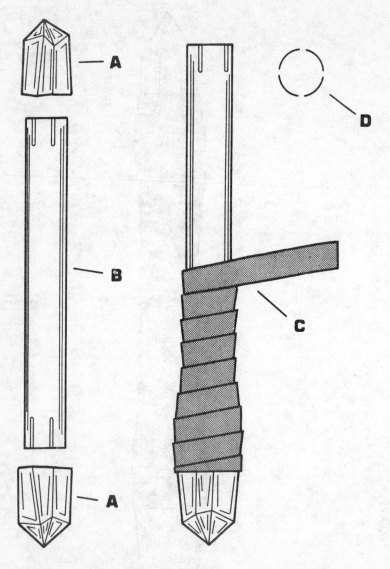

DOUBLE CRYSTAL HEALING ROD
  A. Quartz Crystals
  B. Copper Pipe (tube, cylinder, etc.)
  C. Leather Wrap (glued-on insulation)
  D. Notched Copper Tube Ends

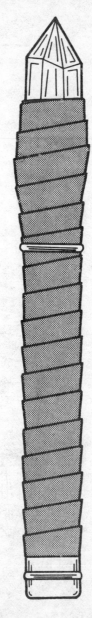

SINGLE CRYSTAL POWER ROD

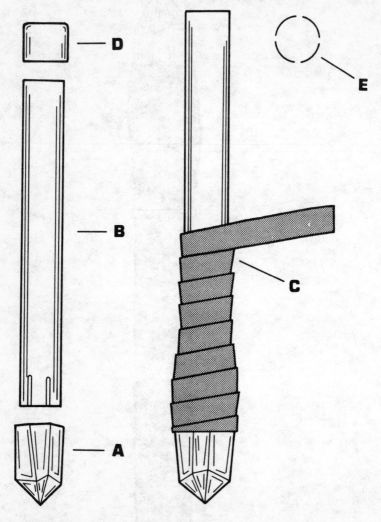

SINGLE CRYSTAL POWER ROD
A. Quartz Crystal
B. Copper Tube
C. Copper Cap
E. Notched Copper Tube End

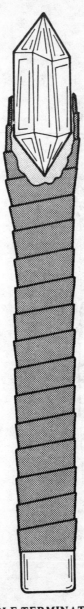

ENERGY ROD WITH DOUBLE TERMINATION QUARTZ CRYSTAL - CUTAWAY VIEW

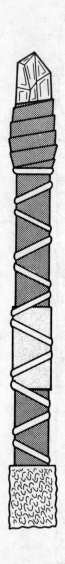

STAFF- LONGER VERSION OF STANDARD ENERGY ROD

What Now?

The previous descriptions covered the outside of the Power Rods and their construction. Now we will take a journey inside the operator. The journey goes deeper into the workings of the biomagnetic field, the geomagnetic field, and the source: the particle/wave field of the Universe. We are going to take a look at the simultaneous interaction and interrelationship of the human, the planet, and the cosmos. They are all vital parts of the process of using a Power Rod. So vital, in fact, that they are inseparable during the time of action and interaction.

Let's look at the machine—the Power Rod—itself. First, take away all the myths and preconceptions. Take away the mystical tradition. Take away the magical connotations. Look at exactly what it is. It is a miniature linear accelerator. It is a 12" long subatomic particle beam generator.

Most of the linear accelerators you've heard of in the last 20 years are the mile-long and even two-mile long monsters at the physics laboratories. Now, it wasn't much more than 20 years ago that a computer filled a 3-story building. Today you can buy one and hold it in your hand. You've heard that particle accelerator experiments took millions of dollars to finance. Not long ago, that was true of computers. Today you can buy or build one for a few thousand or even a few hundred dollars.

Why do you think particle beam generators have not been advertised to the public? The reasons for this may or may not be obvious. Linear accelerators or subatomic particle beam generators are the most powerful machines ever built by man. Many subatomic particles travel at almost the speed of light. They also travel through all materials: earth, wood, metal, concrete, deep space. Everything in existence is composed of atoms and their substructure, subatomic particles. We live and move and have our being in a vast sea (the Universe) of subatomic particles. These particles, waves, and fields are the ever-changing forces of creation in motion. They are the basis of all creation and of all destruction, as well.

These particles make up everything we see: tables, cars, houses, plants, animals, everything we are, or have, or build, or buy. This is the force of the world, and that includes us, personally. In fact, there is no way to separate ourselves from this process, the ever-changing Universe. Regardless of philosophy or religion, we are all intimately involved. If there are other people dealing with this on an everyday, routine basis, maybe we should also be directly, consciously involved.

Particles change; we change. We change our thoughts, our feelings, our bodies. Everything we come in contact with changes on a particle level; sometimes slow, sometimes fast. With the use of an Energy Rod, we are taking an active part in the process of universal change. Not only that, we have every right to do so. How much or how fast is totally up to us as individuals. If you and I are alive, we have certain inalienable universal rights by the fact that we exist.

When an operator of an Energy Rod picks one up, his or her biomagnetic field immediately begins working the rod. The rod accumulates particles (energy) in the copper chamber (cylinder). It begins building as soon as the operator touches the rod. The intensity of the accumulated energy is dependent on the emotions of the operator as he or she uses the rod.

After the rod is charged, the focus is controlled by the thoughts/mind projections of the operator. Whatever the operator is focusing on or thinking of is where the energy in the rod will go. Although this requires some concentration and visualization by the person using the rod, it does not need as much as you might think. That's where the programmed machine part comes into play. While complete control is the responsibility of the individual, the machine does amplify and augment the particles created by the thoughts of the person using it.

A person's thought does create in the form of particles/waves and energy fields an effect on the world around them. This has been explained in many courses dealing with positive thinking, goal setting, and self-improvement. In a slower fashion, thought helps us attain jobs, houses, cars, and the many other things we want out of life.

Let's suppose you want to change the world around you with an Energy Rod. How about an Energy Rod for healing? A family pet has just been wounded in a fight. This friendly tomcat has some cuts and bites and open wounds on his front leg. Rather than see him suffer, you would want to help him get well as fast as possible.

While the cat is sleeping (since he isn't likely to hold still while you're using an Energy Rod on him), move the rod around his body in a clockwise circle to add positive energy to his biomagnetic (body's) field. Feel and visualize the energy in the rod beaming into the area of his body. Mentally be aware of the energy from your body flowing through the rod. The whole area, from the ground up, is a field of force being tapped as it flows through your body. Think of the energy of the Earth's magnetic field flowing from the ground and the lines of Earth force about six feet above the ground. As you imagine this, think of the particles and waves of energy flowing in from the rest of the Universe. Feel them flowing to you, the Earth, through the rod, while beaming to the field around the cat's body. This takes longer to write and read about than it does to do.

Now that you've done this, aim the rod at the cat's hurt leg and think of the healing energy flowing into the injured part, doing it's healing work. Do this from five to ten feet away so that you don't wake up the cat—the cat may feel the energy and wake up anyway. If he does, just wait until he goes to sleep again; then, start the same process all over again. It will take some patience. As you continue to think of the beam of energy flowing into the hurt area, think of any infection being eliminated and the body's healing and closing the wound. Imagine the blue-white light, flowing, surrounding the injured area. Do you feel a tingling sensation of warmth from the area? Sometimes you feel it and sometimes you don't. If you do feel it, the area will cool off when the healing is done.

This cooling effect is a good thing to watch for because it tells you that you've done enough for one treatment. More treatments may be necessary over a period of time for maximum healing effects or if the bone has been broken. In that case, after the veterinarian has treated the cat, use the rod to help the bone knit together faster. Think of that as you are using the rod to send positive energy to the cat's body.

Practice usually improves the process. The more you use it, the better it works. Many people are able to work it well with little or no practice at all and you may be one of them.

The healing process can be used on plants, animals and people. In the case of people or animals, it is wise to have them treated by their doctor or veterinarian, as well as using your Healing Rod to help them recover. This is one of the most positive effects that can come from Energy Rod usage.

What happens during other uses of Power Rods? Examples may help our understanding of the entire interrelationship between us, the rod, the Earth, the Universe, and the interacting particles/waves/fields of energy of all. Some of the examples referred to are for outright combat, weather influence, and similar unconventional uses. While the action and energy can be the same, we should examine both the similarities and the differences.

The uses of the Power Rod by the warrior is obviously a stressful one. However, it's probably good to have some understanding of the combat mode of operation. The warrior with a Combat Power Rod (a black leather-wrapped one) has one purpose in mind—to stop the enemy. This may be with the intention to incapacitate or to kill or withdraw the energy field from the adversary's body permanently. In either case, the attitude is extremely intense for the Power Rod operator.

The emotional energy for combat, the extreme mental energy, is related to the operator's central nervous system, combined with the biochemistry that produces and releases adrenalin. The stress in this type of operation can be almost unbearable.

Some people are well adapted to this; some people are definitely not suited to it at all. When a warrior goes into a battle, he or she usually knows it ahead of time. This emotional buildup is the reaction of survival instinct. During the time leading up to the battle, this energy increases many times over. In fact, the Power Rod as a point of concentration helps the operator to focus on the act of bringing energy into the physical realm. A great deal of practice or experience is usually required for the control necessary to keep thoughts focused on the energy from the stars, Earth, buildup of energy in the rod, and then the release of the beam toward its target.

Some people are able to do this almost automatically. They may be the warriors of the past or the warriors of the future. They can easily see, in their minds, the power penetration of an enemy's shield and body's energy field. They can, without a doubt in their minds, sweep away an opponent's very life force. That is usually their intention. Very few, if any, ever intend to just paralyze an adversary. Some of the greatest warriors can, and do, but it is a rare occurrence nowadays.

One of the most powerful stimulations for the warrior mode is the position of being outnumbered or in an almost impossible position. The warrior uses all the emotional energy of fear, as well as other feelings of the time, to amplify her/his own force. At a time when there seems to be no other alternatives, their minds are freed from self-limitations, allowing them to achieve impossible acts of power. These attitudes are then magnified hundreds of times over as they create the particle/waves of energy flowing through the Power Rods. I don't really want to recommend this type of use to anyone.

I would recommend that if you learn the combat use of the Combat Power Rod, you reserve it for extreme emergencies under very adverse conditions: only if our world situation becomes practically impossible to handle with any other means.

Knowledge itself is a powerful form of stored energy. Wisdom and self-control are very important in relation to any type of Power Rods. That's especially true of this one.

Let's take a look at weather and its influence by particle beam generators. In this operation, there is far less stress on the operator. Clouds, rainmaking, storms, and winds are mentioned frequently in many myths and traditions. Can they really be created and influenced by people? It may be best to experiment in order to find out for yourself.

It seems reasonable to expect that most of the Earth's weather is controlled and influenced by the Earth's own magnetic (particle/wave) field, with the exception of the influence from solar electromagnetic radiation and even some intersteller radiation. Most control is with the Earth itself. If man wanted to influence the Earth's weather, it is logical that he would start with the planet's own geomagnetic field. That's exactly where we'll start, using the Power Rod for an interaction with it.

Back to square one; the operator's biomagnetic field is already intimately connected with the geomagnetic field. Insert a force of influence, intensify and focus energy specifically into the already existing patterns, through the circuits or connections, that are in place by nature. If it sounds familiar, it is because we're using the same energy process to achieve different results. The operator of the Energy Rod must first be able to picture exactly the kind of weather conditions he or she wants to create or influence.

A true test would be to form clouds in a desert area during a clear day in Summer. Visualize the energy of the Earth flowing up from the ground and through you. At the same time, visualize the energy of the Sun and the stars flowing down from the sky through the top of your head. Continue to picture the movement of the blue-white light energy flowing through your body, through your arm, into the Power Rod, and building up a charge in the copper chamber behind the quartz crystal.

When you get the feeling that you're ready, imagine the energy being released in a narrow beam pointing up into the sky and spreading out into a cloud at a reasonable altitude. Picture the type of cloud you want—just one small one at first. Different types of clouds form at different heights. You may want to refer to a book that shows the different types of clouds or you may want to give yourself a better idea of their form by observing naturally-formed clouds for several weeks before you try this experiment.

Another good idea is to practice visualizing clouds in your mind's eye for a few days before the experiment in order to form a clearer conception of what you want to create. I'd recommend nice white puffy cumulus clouds as a good first attempt at this procedure. They're pleasant to look at. They are also harmless and unthreatening, as well. Be careful with what you try to create at first.

After an adequate amount of practice and experience, you may want to carry this project a few steps further by projecting the image of darker clouds. By the time you reach this point, visualizing thunder and lightning along with the clouds is a relatively easy step. In the case of wind, the process is the same. You can advance this procedure as far as you are capable of.

Let's take a closer look at the Energy Rod effects on our present-day society. Considering that our entire society is based on electromagnetic radiation (particles and waves), it's balanced on a very fine line. Electricity is electromagnetic radiation under our control, at least the part we don't waste. The invisible forces we take for granted every day are tremendous. They are also vulnerable by their very nature. The simple fact is this: any system that runs on particles, like electricity (the particles are electrons), can be influenced by another system using particles. I mean they are really sensitive to other particle or radiation field influences. In fact, many of the systems in use today are so sensitive to the fields of other systems that they have to be shielded from other systems in the same room, or even the same building.

All subatomic particles are extremely sensitive to external influences. Therein lies the key to our Universe. Subatomic particles react to influences from other forms of energy and/or matter. All forms of energy and matter are composed entirely of the same types of subatomic particles in various arrangements.

Our minds, our very thoughts, can easily influence these subatomic particles. Our thoughts create and transmute all the different types of particles into other types of particles. It's considered quite difficult to move things around with mind power alone. Telekinesis is a feat you'd think could only be accomplished by experienced psychics, or you may think it's all just a fraud or a parlor trick. Every object is composed of subatomic particles. Your self-doubt about whether it really works may keep you from ever moving an object.

Your mind moves particles around everyday. If you think of moving a whole table, it may not move. If you think of a particle or particles, they move and they move fast. Some of them, with just a thought, will move at almost the speed of light. The catch is, you move them all the time; you just may not see them move. Particles are also in a state of constant movement themselves. It requires very little mental influence to change their course or pattern. It really is a lot easier if you happen to have a machine to augment and amplify your thoughts about doing these things.

You and an Energy Rod can easily affect changes in our world. Not just subtle changes in thinking, but radical, physical changes. You can do it right now, anywhere on this Earth. What you do is up to you. What I do is up to me. We both have the same Universal Human Rights to do according to the best of our knowledge and understanding.

What in the world can you do with an Atlantean Power Rod, now, in our present society? You can do whatever you can think of while you have the knowledge and power to do so.

This is an electrical-based society. Practically everything we have, use, and do, is now dependent on the most common type of subatomic particle: the electron. Our electricity is only the flow of electrons along wires; to every computer, every house, every business, airplane, space shuttle, every missile and warhead, through the electrical systems of our cars and trucks, ovens, TV sets, typewriters, washers, dryers and radios. In the electron particle flow we live. In the electron particle flow, we can, and probably will, change, grow, expand, reach out and touch the rest of the world. Most of the particle systems we would touch right now are totally unshielded from our direct, personal, individual influence. This is especially true if we are using the high-powered energy equipment described in this book.

Power Rods have been in the possession of some public and/or private citizens, like you and I, for slightly less than a decade. Very few people have built them and even fewer people are using them. That is changing, even as you read this. People are using them in the way human nature uses everything that people come into contact with. These rods are being used to:

1. Alter electric systems such as traffic lights.
2. Alter computer systems in all areas where they are used.
3. Influence automobile engines and systems.
4. Influence weapons systems such as tanks, lasers, and aircraft.
5. Influence missiles and nuclear warheads.
6. Influence satellite spy cameras and infrared sensors.
7. Augment positive thinking programs for health and happiness.
8. Amplify sales programs to increase profits from sales.
9. Augment human development practices for both individuals and groups.
10. Stop harmful practices such as human rights

violations.

11. Influence world religions in order to promote peace.
12. Increase beneficial results in scientific research.
13. Increase medical efficiency for healing practices.
14. Influence weather for increased crop/food production.
15. Increase accurate predictability for future conditions.
16. Induce positive plant growth for food and beauty.
17. Increase manufacturing/productivity for positive growth.
18. Increase basic human development to keep up with the growth of our technology.
19. Promote space exploration and development for peaceful purposes.
20. Intensify the communication with intelligent extraterrestrial life.

Picture a dark night, a desolate stretch of highway somewhere in the Southern United States, and a middle-aged man on his way home. He stops his car in stunned silence as he sees a saucershaped craft 50 yards away. There are some human forms apparently working at something underneath the saucer. He gets out of his car and starts to approach the strange scene. One of the alien figures turns, pointing a metallic rod with a clear crystal which emits a pencil-thin beam of blue/white light at him. He feels a tingling sensation as his body is paralyzed. Hours later the paralysis wears off; the flying saucer has gone. He doesn't know what to do. Who is going to believe a story like that, anyway?

Suffering from ovarian cysts, a housewife in her early 20s living in the Western United States has gone to a psychic healer for help with her medical problem. Holding a copper and leather wrapped rod (with crystals in both ends), the 30-year old psychic carefully traces the outline of the patient's body and then concentrates on the affected midsection. After only 25 minutes, the treatment is completed.

Three weeks later, the housewife's medical doctor's x-rays show that all of the cysts have disappeared. Another successful treatment with ancient technology.

In Arizona, a hot rod is roaring down the street. Several teenagers are laughing as they pass through a yellow traffic light. One of them is holding a Power Rod which he has just focused on the light. He's caused it to stay yellow for eight minutes. He thinks it's great fun.

In an apartment in New York, a 12-year old boy is amazing his young friends by moving a compass needle from a distance of 3 feet. He's doing it with an Energy Rod he built of copper and a quartz crystal. He's never done anything like this before.

A 60-year old, gray-haired woman living in San Francisco is talking to her plants. As she does, she points a Crystal Rod at them to increase their growth. In the last 3 months, they've nearly doubled in size!

These are only a few of the examples and possibilities available for positive growth, for ourselves as individuals and for our society, which may one day grow enough to finally be called a true civilization.

CHAPTER THREE

SUBATOMICS AND PSIONICS: THOUGHT CREATION

"If we could think of a way to convert mass to energy with 100% efficiency, we could produce power for all the homes, cars, factories—everything on the whole planet—from one ten pound lump of coal, for one day, and still have some left over for the next day. Energy efficiency has not been seriously considered yet!"

Psionics involves the projection of an effect from a mental image, with the person acting as the first cause. In the early psionic machines invented in the late 1940's, the image was generally a photograph or a sample. Using electronic parts and patterns for their operation, these early-generation machines are still being built and used today. There are some good books on the market giving the details of the first black boxes patented in the late 1940's and 50's (see Suggested Reading List).

Newer generation psionics use a much faster method which by-passes the photographs and sample plates. In the 1980's devices, there are patterns and shapes still involved, but they have discarded most electronic parts.

The relationship psionics holds, other than with the human mind, is that it deals with particles/waves/fields. There are a few good books available on the new physics which parallel subatomic particle wave and field physics (see Suggested Reading List). These are written for the layman, and not in mathematical terms. They cover the basics of particle and field theories. You may want to read some of them for general information relating to some of the practices and projects described here.

Nearly all subatomic particles break down or break up as they transmute and transform into different types of other particles. It's been said that when an electron goes backward in time, it gets a new name—it becomes positron. It's also been said that the positron is also the term for antimatter or an anti-electron.

The atom is composed of protons, neutrons, and electrons. All of the particles are subject to breakdown and transformation into other kinds of particles. The reason so many new subatomic particles are discovered may be due to the possibility that the minds of researchers are creating the particles by the very act of looking at, or for, them. It's been mentioned quite frequently that the machines and the observers influence the actions of the particles. This could certainly mean that the scientists are mentally projecting them and may explain why so many particles have been created in the last few years. It could also explain why physicists always find the postulated particles that they're looking for sooner or later. It may take time, but the imaginary particles are found. This may also mean that it takes exactly that amount of time for the concentration of the observer to be focused into a material or energy form.

Yogis or mystics use their minds to create physical forms as part of their training and practice. This may be what is currently being done in the area of physics. Understanding the jumble of new particles is a process that could be continued indefinitely by looking for them while imagining that they exist. This is an unending process and a cycle that will not lead anywhere except to the discovery and naming of new particles.

Applying the particles, waves, and fields that have been discovered is a more productive use of our knowledge and energy. Learning to use, creating, and manipulate the particles we know seems to be a logical step to take. It makes little difference who the particle is named after, or what its weight is, if you can create and send it where you want it to go and get it to do what you want it to do. Many particles travel just slightly below the speed of light; they also travel through all matter. When traveling through cells particles effect changes instantly.

Focusing the mind on sending the particles to a specific destination with a specific task to do will achieve more results than other types of research. It is not necessary to know either the particle's name, position or its velocity in order to influence it and beam it wherever you want it to go. It is helpful to know exactly where you want it to go, however, and what effect you want it to have once the destination is reached.

Psionics appear in many forms. One of the most common is in the form of dowsing. The dowser holds a mental image in his or her mind of the material being searching for. It may be an underground water source, or a specific type of mineral. In this respect, dowsing rods can be said to be other versions of psionic machines. The major active portion is definitely in the mind of the operator. It is the key that institutes and controls the action to be manifested as an end result.

With respect to Energy Rods and Crystal Devices, copper chambers merely accumulate particles and store a charge, while the mind of the operator focuses them through the quartz crystal. As this applies to subatomic particles, the mind of the operator while he or she is focusing this energy is creating, and at the same time altering, some particles. It does change the particle speed, influence their direction and their destination.

Particles do not behave according to standard rules. Subatomic particles have been known to appear at two places simultaneously. Two different particles have been known to follow the same course at the same time, or follow parallel courses to a target. Subatomic particles have been known to move backward and forward in time; past to present to future.

It has been postulated that there are particles that travel faster than the speed of light. It's never been adequately proven yet that you can take a particle traveling slower than the speed of light and accelerate it to faster than light. However, it has been postulated that tachyons (particles moving faster than light) always keep moving faster than light. This is going to make it very hard to catch these in an experimental chamber and look at them. Nonetheless, if they do exist and are traveling faster than light, they can be subject to the influence of the human mind in conjunction with the psionic device. They can be controlled. They can be focused. They can be used.

This is very similar to electricity using electrons. While we've developed quite a technology using electricity, it's still never been adequately defined. What it really is may never be clearly known.

Particles exist naturally; they do not have to be created in a linear accelerator, cloud chamber, or any other device. They are constantly in existence and motion, whether it's the atoms that make up the structures around us, in radiating from the magnetic fields of our bodies or the Earth, coming from the solar system, or from other star systems.

There are literally billions of subatomic particles passing through us and circulating around us at all times during the day. We have constant access to this obviously unlimited source of energy. They are already here; they are already flowing in and around you. Your mind with its thought patterns is already creating them and, therefore, the process of working with particles is already about 90 percent complete. By learning to use psionic subatomic particle devices, you are constructing shapes to collect and focus particles while using the mind and emotions to move these particles in paths to your own predesignated destination.

Imagination and visualization is extremely important to using psionic subatomics. Understanding the concepts

necessary to imagine or visualize may be a little bit confusing at first, i.e. imagining something moving backward in
time may be difficult for some people. It may also be difficult to conceive of one thing being in several different
places at the same time; two identical particles, or one particle, breaking and being in two different places concurrent-
ly. At the same time, it is still within the realm of our self-
control to imagine particles or thought patterns moving
faster than light. We can imagine them accelerating from
slower than light speed to faster than light speed and passing through everything moving out into space at the speed
of light. We are now at the point where our minds can
finally begin to be used in a more productive manner.

In a down-to-earth perspective, our thoughts attract
to us what we want out of life. There are people who can
imagine that they have a newer house, or a better job, or
more money, and the thought patterns create particles that
reach out, latch onto, and attract those sort of things just
like a magnetic field.

This is not something alien to our minds, insomuch as
we use it more every day, many times unconsciously. We
are in the act of creating with our minds at all times. We
are creating particle beams when we concentrate. We are
doing most of the things required to operate a psionic,
subatomic machine, just as a matter of course. It's only a
matter of doing what we normally do as human beings,
only doing it in a more conscious fashion; visualizing the
images a little more clearly; reaching out with our imagination a little bit further, and a little bit faster. We are taking
a natural everyday process and speeding up the time; increasing the scope or distance of the cause and effect relationship. How good we are at this depends on our natural
abilities and talents. It also depends on a great deal of
practice.

There's also a time factor. Time speeds up and slows
down, since time is relative. Think about time. Think about
how much, how fast, and what you want in conjunction
with time. Remember the emotion, the desire and intensity

which can affect time. One person might expect to achieve results in five minutes while using his or her consciousness to influence particles. Another taking the same action in the same way would be described as having a time lag. The same effect may take a week, six weeks, six months, or six years to achieve. The people who get the fastest results are the ones who have an intense desire, or are enthusiastic. This is augmented by the fact that they have learned to expect results; to expect the effects they want. They don't negate the effects with self-doubt or loss of their mental visualization images or control. Their minds and mental processes are working in harmony with their emotional state; their imagination and conception of time is in relationship to it all.

In thinking of what subatomic particles do, take into consideration that they do not always appear as particles. It's easier to think of them this way, but their behavior also indicates that they act as waves, sometimes referred to as the wave/particle duality. In considering particles, we're really dealing with three different things at once. Instead of working with a particle as we might imagine it, we are also looking at a wave that moves out and radiates. These form particle/wave fields. We are dealing with particles, waves, and fields.

Summary

Up to this point, we've looked at the factors involved in using our minds to create things. The main characteristic of this, easier than creation through thought patterns, has been manipulating and controlling the subatomic particle forces that are already in existence, passing through and around us. Admittedly we can add to this and create new particle waves as we think of things while we work with it. The main factor to bear in mind is that we are creating at all times through our thought patterns. The second factor to bear in mind is that we are manipulating already existing patterns at all times. The difference described has been through visualization and clear thoughts. We decide exactly where we want thought, or subatomic, particles to travel and what effects we want them to have. This is the equivalent of instantaneous thought creation and transmission.

We've previously dealt with building the basic machine, the rod, that amplifies and augments this natural thought process and we've described the basic background in a general fashion of how this process works. To summarize, thoughts create particles; particles act as waves and fields. Imagine and visualize a particle traveling through space at almost the speed of light, or traveling faster than light, and acting as a wave and breaking down and fluctuating into fields. This is a holistic way of viewing ourselves in relation to the world around us. This is also a process that continues after we give up our physical body and soul-consciousness (or whatever term you would choose according to your philosophy) leaves the body. We are still in existence within the Universe. This is the type of knowledge and information that we can, and do, take with us into the after-death state. That makes it valuable information, indeed.

Everything created in this Universe, from the time it was created, is still in existence today. Granted, it is in an everchanging state, but it is still in a moving existence and not likely to disappear. This includes ourselves. In long-range planning, most people don't consider what they're going to do after they experience death. While there are many philosophies that deal with reincarnation in a new body and merging with the "One Creative Universal Force", or the "White Light", or "God", let's consider other alternatives.

If you are in an aware and conscious part of this creative process, many other alternatives open up to you. If you know who you are and what you are doing, you can plan far enough ahead to consciously continue being involved in the process. Death becomes perceived as a minor interruption to what you're really doing.

We are always in existence somewhere, doing something so it's a good idea to have a long-range plan to that effect. It's a practical opportunity to take advantage of and use our knowledge to travel throughout other dimensions and realms and to continue the creative process in which we are already involved. It's a beneficial attitude to assume that even if you are dead, you've just been born somewhere else and you'll still be doing something. It may not mean that you've been born in a physical body. It may not mean that you have a brain as you had in this physical body. It does mean that there is a vital part of you that has the imprint of experience and the knowledge to continue actively creating and working with and through this Universe (and the dimensions of this Universe) on a continuous basis. This may be best described as a process that from our limited point of view is never going to end. That's why it would be a good idea to learn how to deal with it until it becomes common practice to think of your mind images, visualizations, and thoughts, as creating particles, waves, and fields, and interacting with the Universe in a dynamic fashion.

CHAPTER FOUR

THE ATLANTEAN CRYSTAL HEADBAND

"There's a whole Universe out there. We ought to know! We created most of it."

Looking back thousands of years ago to the jungles of South America, an already ancient pyramid sits in the center of a stone city on a mountaintop that juts through the clouds. The full moon illuminates the flat platform of the pyramid. A priestess walks up the stairway to the sky. The moonlight reflects off of her white robe and the shiny crystal headband she carries. As she reaches the top, she glances toward the stars while placing the crystal crown around her head. The crystal and silver shine like a diamond on her forehead. She closes her eyes. Her vision turns inward, seeking to communicate with the ancient ones who came from the stars in the time of her ancestors. As she thinks of the seven sisters of the star cluster (later to be known as the Plieades), she remembers stories her grandmother told her of the great cities and wonders of the Sky people. What does the future hold for her people? She is hoping for answers from the revered Star Council that sent its people to colonize her home planet, the Earth, in the ancient times.

Little remains of this past, aside from the ruins of the pyramids—except for one thing, the crown of copper, crystal and silver. The Crystal Headband was the only link between people in the days of old when the distance between the colonies was measured in light years instead of miles. The knowledge of how to build this was not completely lost for all time; it has now been returned to us. An artifact renewed in our time. With it has come some understanding of how to use it, but not all. Only experience will bring it al back to us. Perhaps it will bring back other things of value as well. For now, it may be enough to build and begin to use the Atlantean Crystal Headband again.

This has been spoken of as a device to amplify thoughts. It focuses and beams these to a specific destination, dependent on the operator. The quartz crystal, in conjunction with the copper band and silver disc, acts as a capacitor for storing the energy and a transducer for changing its form. Thoughts and images are converted at the speed of light into beams which are sent to a receiver at some distance or time. The receiver again converts the stream of particles back into images, thoughts, and emotions. This is not any different than the principles involved in radio and television, except the machine is simpler and more sophisticated with an increased number of the energy workings dependent on the individual and naturally occurring particle fields. The process is very similar to those we are already familiar with.

I hesitate to use the term "psychic", since it is a limited concept, but this device does augment psychic impressions. In many cases, this can be extremely helpful; or, it can also be disorienting and confusing. Until you become adept with its use, it can amplify emotions and thoughts inside you that are not the ones you had planned on using. This is why I recommend adopting the most positive attitude you can achieve while operating the Headband. Like anything else we build and use, it can be used in a positive or negative manner. Positive is more fun and productive.

That there are intelligent forms of life out in space is a probability, and it is also likely that there are some that are more advanced than we are. In short, they're not trying to call you on the phone or radio. A reasonable assumption is that they would use the most efficient energy and process available: simple mental projection.

There are some great stories floating around about intelligent and advanced beings who communicate mentally as a matter of routine, daily experience. We may be growing in that direction, but as of now, we need to assist ourselves with sophisticated mind machines as the first steps are taken. That's what the copper/silver/crystal Headband is for—sending and receiving thoughts and impressions.

The Headband is a relatively simple device with no moving parts. It is composed of a copper band with a silver disc and a clear-tipped quartz crystal on top of the silver disc. That's it—easy to construct with a few tools and some patience.

The hand tools needed are:

A pair of pliers.

A pair of tin snips.

A tube of instant-bonding glue.

A small file.

A small drill.

The materials needed are:

1. A sheet of thin copper (to be cut and bent to form the band). This is available from a sheet metal company, hobby, or hardware store.
2. A one ounce silver disc or coin (available from a coin shop or dealer).
3. A quartz crystal about 1½" long and ¾" to 1" in diameter (available from most rock shops, it should have a clear, unchipped tip).
4. Two narrow strips of leather, about a foot long for each, 1/8" to ¼" wide.

The construction begins by cutting the copper sheet to form a band. Refer to the diagram for the basic shape. Leave enough extra copper on the front to bend around and form to the crystal. Please be careful of any sharp edges until you file them smooth as you shape and fit the band. You may want to pinch the base of the crystal with the pliers to break off any rough or pointed edges. Be careful not to crack the crystal itself.

After the crystal is ready, start bending the copper piece on the front of the band to fit and hold the crystal. If the crystal you have has one side that is flatter than the others, place that flat side against the copper. Bend the copper around the crystal for the tightest fit possible. You may have to take the crystal out and bend the copper with your pliers several times to get a good fit. You'll find it will still be slightly loose.

The next step is to slide the silver disc in behind the crystal. It should fit tightly between the crystal and the copper band. If it doesn't, refit the crystal. If the silver disc does fit well with the crystal, place a few drops of instant-bonding glue around the crystal, the silver disc, and the copper band. This should seal the band tightly together for a permanent final fit.

Next, at the rounded ends of the band (they should have been filed smooth earlier), drill a small hole at each end for the leather strips to fit through. Tie knots in one end of each leather strip; a bead or two can be added to make sure the strips don't pull through the holes in the band. These two thongs are for tying the Headband on and adjusting it to fit. You are now ready to try out your recreated Atlantean Crystal Headband.

Find, or create, a quietly peaceful environment similar to a place you would use for meditation, prayer, or psychic readings. Assume a position that is comfortable for your body. This may be lying down, sitting in a chair or on the ground or floor. Peace and comfort are the key elements at first. When you are relaxed, place the Headband on your head and adjust the fit ′as you center the silver disc/crystal on your forehead, with the point of the crystal up.

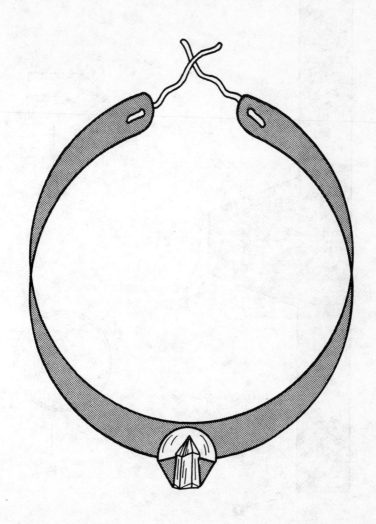

ATLANTEAN CRYSTAL HEADBAND

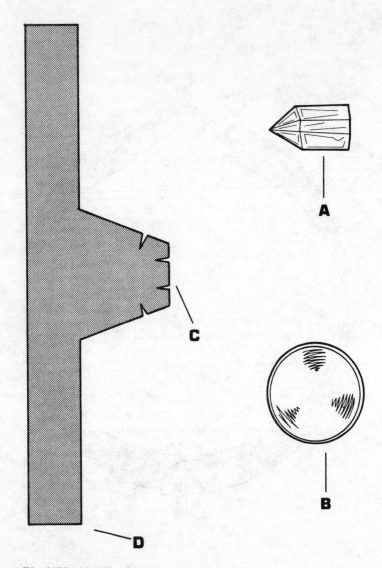

ATLANTEAN CRYSTAL HEADBAND

    A. Quartz Crystal
    B. Silver Disc
    C. Slots for Bending to mount crystal
    D. Corners (cut off rounded)

You are now sitting or lying quietly waiting for something to happen. What? If your mind isn't focused on something in particular, you'll probably feel some confusing sensations. The first test of the Headband sometimes causes a feeling of disorientation. This is usually a variety of mixed feelings, such as dizziness, confusion, and even headaches. These aren't always experienced, but can be until you are attuned to the Headband. This takes time and practice.

After the first time you try it, wait awhile. When you try again, think of the specific action you desire. What do you want? Do you intend to receive psychic impressions? If so, focus your thoughts on and visualize the subject you you expect information about. Do you want to communicate with someone at a distance? If this is the case, it's better at first to try communicating with a close friend or a member of your family where a strong connection already exists. If you want to find out about an object or person, picture the subject in your mind as clearly as you can. Do you want to send a thought message? Are you trying to receive a message from someone else?

After you become experienced with this device, you might want to see how far you can go. You may be tempted to pick up communications from someone out in space at another place in the Universe. It's a natural curiosity for us and can take some doing until you run into people who are expecting to hear from you on a regular basis. After that, you'll probably have an idea of at least which star system you are communicating with.

After some more experience, you may even have a clear idea of the person with whom you are communicating, a visual impression and even a name. This will seem a bit strange at first. Think of it as you would about talking on the telephone. It's just using a different machine, that's all. And of course it can really be long distance. At first, I would suggest limiting your activities to Earth people. After you feel confident with this, get rid of your own self-limitations and restrictions. You will find it possible to do whatever you think you can do from here on.

If people knew this was so easy and economical, they'd probably want to communicate with other people all over the Universe just for fun and knowledge. That's the most important practice that I think there is—learning as much about ourselves and our world as we can.

Everybody has latent psychic and mental talents they can develop with patience and practice. You can do this with a Crystal Headband. Communication with other beings in your Universe can be accomplished using the same techniques. There are a few things to remember when you are communicating with someone in space. Remember that they are people; they are not different than anyone else. Some are pretty nice; some are not so good; some are just plain indifferent or apathetic. Ask the same logical questions of anyone you meet that you would if you met some new friends here. Ask who they are, where they are, and what they do. If they try to feed you a line by pretending to be the greatest of something or other, tell them to take a hike. Don't put up with a bunch of bull, even from supposedly advanced beings from another part of space. After all, you're a reasonably advanced being from part of space, this part. If there's ever a time to be "down to earth", this is the time. Sounds ironic, doesn't it? Simply use common sense.

The same thing applies to psychic phenomena: use common sense. If someone claims they are so and so who does this or that, ask who, what, how, and where. Remember to lighten up a bit when you're dealing with this. It doesn't make any difference who you are talking to. Be yourself—hopefully with a good sense of humor.

Running into a space version of Will Rogers is entirely possible. In fact, that would be a good experience for those of us who tend to be too serious-minded.

A 35-year old woman psychic in Chicago has just placed a copper Headband around her head. On the front of her forehead is a silver disc with a quartz crystal in the center. She's starting to feel slightly dizzy now, but the impressions are coming in. She's determined to get used to the thought amplifier. She constructed the device herself from instructions a friend gave her. She feels familiar with the Headband; it feels like something she used in a previous lifetime. The swirls of light are forming into clear impressions in her mind as she relaxes. Could this be your experience, too?

The younger "Star Wars/Video Game Generation" generally finds this much more acceptable to deal with. Their conception of space, time and people is probably somewhat more expanded than ours.

CHAPTER FIVE

SUPERMINDS IN ACTION

"Sometimes I wonder about the search for intelligent life in outer space. It has never been proven that intelligent life exists on this planet."

What is a Supermind? It has been a subject of myth and tradition, science fiction and fantasy stories, that Superminds exist. We picture highly evolved beings, usually surrounded by an aura of white light, white-robed, gray-haired, bearded, with wisdom beyond our present conception. We imagine there are advanced civilizations in our Universe where the people have evolved far beyond anything we could think of at present. What would be the characteristics of a super-evolved being? Or beings from a far-advanced civilization that's had millions of years more to grow and develop than we have had on Earth?

The main characteristic of such a mind, or such a being, would be the development of the being, itself, beyond technology. It's interesting to note that in our present society, the frontiers of science have reached the edge of material technology. In delving into the makeup of the atom and its particles, researchers and scientists have discovered the sub-Universe, often referred to as the microcosm (the other Universe is the macrocosm). Scientists have gone past particles into the micron world; to the edge of a Universe that is so small they are looking into the sub-structure, beyond subatomic particles. We've reached the point in our technology where the miniature circuits in electronics and computers are refined to such a small size that they use practically no energy at all to function. Layer upon layer of circuits have been laid across silicon crystals. A particle, or an atom, might be only a few microns or less across.

The next step beyond the discoveries made in the sub-micron Universe does not lead to a further development of smaller technology. At the point where technology is being developed from subatomic particle research, the next stage of development leads back to the originators (the human minds of the researchers themselves) of the subatomic particle Universe. Our society and its technology has arrived at the foundation for our own development into Super-minds, or super-evolved beings, that we've always imagined existed somewhere else. This is the path that any civilization (who didn't destroy itself through its own faults and thinking processes) in the Universe would follow.

It's been reported that searching for intelligent life in the Universe with radio telescopes and x-ray telescopes, trying to pickup different pulsars and waves being emitted from different systems and looking for a pattern, would indicate that there was intelligent life there. Anyone who reached the foundation of efficiency by exploring the sub-Universe of subatomic particles (or the micron Universe) would have reached the point where they wouldn't use radio or television waves to communicate across space. They would use the direct efficiency method.

As our technology has progressed, and hopefully people along with it, it's become more efficient in that it's simpler instead of more complex. It has become more direct, with less use of energy, instead of moving in the opposite direction to high voltage equipment. We are using lower voltages and duplicating natural processes, such as the biomagnetic and geo.nagnetic fields.

An advanced being from another civilization would not send radio waves. Beings of this nature and this stage of advanced development would communicate consciousness to consciousness; being to being; mind to mind. Simply because this would be the most efficient means possible, the advanced being of myth and tradition, science fiction and fantasy, in reality would be communicating with other beings across time and space with thought particle beams. An advanced being, or a Supermind, would reach out across the interstellar distances by directing subatomic particles through the micron, to the submicron structure, and reaching out, traveling at the speed of light, in some cases, and by using particles traveling faster than light, in other cases, to contact and communicate with other beings.

across time and space with thought particle beams. An advanced being, or a Supermind, would reach out across the interstellar distances by directing subatomic particles through the micron, to the submicron structure, and reaching out, traveling at the speed of light, in some cases, and by using particles traveling faster than light, in other cases, to contact and communicate with other beings.

To someone who has not reached this stage and was using technology such as x-rays, radio telescopes, or television, it would appear that the Universe was uninhabited. There would appear to be no communications traveling back and forth, because the wrong type of technology was being used. The ultimate forms of technology is mind technology, the consciousness and awareness technology. Beings developed to this point would consider it routine to reach out with their minds and explore the Universe without building spaceships or life support systems for their bodies.

Understanding their relationship to the Universe in which they live, formed into blocks or magnetic fields that we call matter, they would have access to any area, any other being, life form, or material in the Universe, regardless of space and distance or time. People who had reached this stage of development would be ready to take a quantum leap in growth and development, mentally and emotionally, because of the feedback and input of knowledge and information gained by reaching out and exploring the

Universe themselves.

As I've mentioned before, the process and connections are already there. The transmission lines, if we wish to think of them as that, are already installed through the particles, waves, and fields of the interconnecting and interrelating Universe. It remains only for us to grow to the point where we know how to operate the ultimate technology.

Over and over again in many philosophies it has been said "look within", which sounds simple, but is no easy feat. However, by looking within ourselves and the submicron Universe, we can finally visualize the concept that we are One and we are interconnected and interrelated to everything else.

The next stage of our development on Earth is to learn to use the knowledge and methods available to us to reach out and explore. At the same time, we will start to realize our potential as co-creators of this Universe, and to recognize the fact we are constantly creating and recreating not only the world around us, but we are constantly creating and recreating the Universe itself, whether it be 400 light years away, across the Galaxy, or through intergalactic relationships. We are intimately connected and are in action with it at all times.

We are, in fact, growing into the Super Beings that we've always imagined existed. It is no longer a matter of "they" being off somewhere else in the Universe. It is a matter of ourselves being what we sought to contact all along. By using the type of technology described in this book, we are stimulating our own growth into mental and emotional giants, which is our next stage of evolution. This means we are taking a conscious, aware and active part in choosing what we will evolve into.

The Supermind is really a being who can control and develop his or her own mind and emotions to a high degree. Instead of looking outside ourselves for the Superminds of the Universe, we should look inside ourselves at this point in our evolution and we will find that we are them!

CHAPTER SIX

CRYSTAL SPACE/TIME
COMMUNICATIONS GENERATOR

*"Universe! You really want to know the secrets of
the Universe? Well, for heavens sake, which one?"*

A New Zealand man is looking at a copper disc with a
large quartz crystal in the center, engaged in his own personal research into the unknown. He's found it to be both
simple and economical. Excitement and purpose have been
added to his life.

It is the late 1970's. In a friend's home, a group of
people are sitting in a circle in the livingroom. In the
middle of the circle on the carpet is a shiny copper disc,
about one foot in diameter. Centered on the disc is a large
quartz crystal, nearly seven inches high, four inches in dia-
mater, and mounted in a round copper cylinder. The sharp
point of the crystal is almost clear as it reflects light like a
prism, breaking it into the colors of the rainbow.

The people sit quietly, connecting the circle by joining
hands and visualizing a blue-white light beacon emanating
from the tip of the power crystal, beaming out into space.
Their project is to make contact with another race of beings
four hundred light years away in the Plieades star cluster (a
large group of stars in the constellation Taurus), densely
packed with over 1200 stars. This seems to be a likely place
to search for an advanced civilization. Attempting to communicate with the star people, these friends are learning
much about themselves.

Extraterrestrial communications as a hobby? Could be interesting. It could be the most important use of this psionic/subatomic machine. Successful extraterrestrial communication on a regular basis could lead to the knowledge we need to survive and grow into our next stage of evolution. This is especially true if our next stage is to be a consciously self-created period.

Assuming there were numerous intergalactic civilizations existing throughout the Universe, what would be the first thing they would trade with each other? Precious gems and metals? Works of art? Weapons? Manufactured goods? All of these are valuable commodities, but there is one commodity worth more than all of these together: knowledge and/or information.

The space traveling free traders of fantasy stories are fictionalized. Most of the portrayed "for trade" items could really be produced by almost any civilization advanced enough to engage in star travel. Many raw materials could easily be synthesized if they weren't already available. What couldn't be produced artificially would be new knowledge/information. That would cover a wider area than any trade goods ever could.

Knowledge and experience is the most important product of any people who exists or who have ever existed. It's the product we want to trade. We talked about space communications earlier just for the fun of it. Here's a practical application. Free enterprise and trade at its finest occurs over instellar distances. Isn't it a reasonable assumption that some of the information we've been talking about was acquired that way?

Let's take a look at building and using a device that many are already using for the purpose of acquiring more knowledge: the quartz Crystal Space/Time Communications Generator, a simple psionic/subatomic machine that has absolutely no moving parts. So sophisticated is this device that the only thing that moves in and through it is energy, but it moves very far and very fast, as you will see.

What travels faster than the speed of light? Thought

or tachyon subatomic particles (waves), that's what. Thoughts instantly produce. Whether they go on to manifest or materialize into energy forms depends entirely on the degree of the thinker.

You and I are the thinkers here, so let's think about building this machine. The basic parts are:

1. One solid copper plate or disc approximately one foot in diameter.
2. One large quartz crystal, three inches in diameter, and about six inches tall.
3. One copper cup.

The copper plate and cup are available at many stores. The copper plate can be replaced with a disc cut from a copper sheet, if that's more convenient. The plain solid copper cylinder can be a copper mug (with the top and handle cut off).

Bend the cup to fit the shape of the crystal and push the crystal base down inside the cup. It should make for a tight fit if the crystal and the cup are roughly the same size. You now have two components, the crystal in the copper base, and the copper disc (or place). Find and mark the center of the disc and glue or weld the bottom of the cup to the center. After the glue sets (glue is easier to use), this device is completed.

The tools necessary for this construction are the same as for the ones we discussed before:

A pair of pliers.

A hacksaw.

A pair of tin snips or shears.

A tube of instant-bonding glue.

A hammer may be necessary to chip off any rough areas at the base of the crystal. If this is needed, please wear safety glasses while you're doing it.

A file may be needed to smooth any sharp edges of the copper cup and disc.

PLEASE NOTE: If the crystal turns out to have a smaller diameter than the cup you're using, you may want to cut small strips of leather to place between the sides of the cup and the crystal. Glue them in as fillers in order to make a tighter fit. Use your own judgment in fitting that part.

When you've finished assembling this, you may find that the quartz crystal does not point straight up from the center of the plate/disc. If it's almost straight, this will work fine. If it's too much out of alignment, you may want to refit the crystal in the copper cup. Again, use your own judgment.

The most promising use for this device is as a space communicator. To make the best possible use of this instrument, you'll need other people. Although you could use it by yourself, the Crystal Headband can be used as easily for the same purpose. For a perfect balance of the polarities involved, two men and two women will provide the best combination as operators. There can be six, eight, or more operators, without worrying about the balance of polarity. Again, this is for you to decide.

It is better to have an imbalance in polarity (sexes) than it is to include someone in the operators' circle who has a negative or otherwise inharmonious attitude. Two people of the same or opposite sexes can also learn to operate this machine adequately, if necessary.

If there are several people operating the communicator, the opportunities for cross-checking any information you receive will make accurate communication more likely. Sometimes, at first, information is received in bits and pieces. Several people can compare and correlate these to produce the complete message or messages. It's a good idea to check and recheck the information.

The mechanics of operation are relatively easy. This communication unit requires an area of floor space on a rug or carpet that can accommodate the number of people who have chosen to use it. Peace and quiet with no likelihood of interruptions is advisable. Dark or light, day or night, it makes no difference. Choose the environment that feels comfortable to you and your friends.

Sit in a circle around the device and join hands in order to form a closer unit in the first attempts at operation.

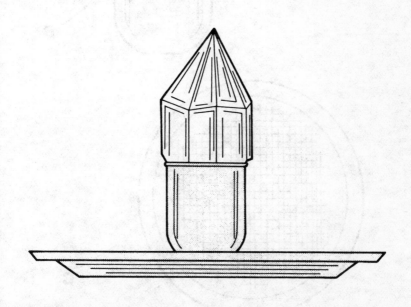

CRYSTAL COMMUNICATION UNIT

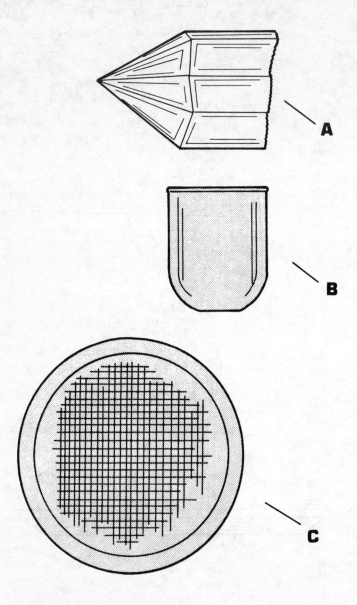

CRYSTAL COMMUNICATION UNIT
   A. Large Quartz Crystal
   B. Copper Cup (cylinder)
   C. Copper Plate

Later on, as you all become more practiced at this, joining hands may not be necessary, depending on the feelings of the group. Sit quietly while closing your eyes.

One person may want to act as the coordinator of the group. If this is the case, the coordinator may want to speak out loud of the purpose of the communication. A verbal description of the area of the stars you are trying to contact may also be helpful. As experience progresses, the coordinator may want to speak of the people you are communicating with as a group or as individuals with names, just as you would if you were using a telephone.

Again, use your own judgment in these matters. In order to bring the operation "down to earth" in a more practical fashion, you may want to visualize yourselves and project your names and images to whomever you are communicating with. Remember, most people you contact are going to be just as interested in you as you are in them!

Further verification of these operations can be accomplished by asking specific questions. For example, ask how to build or invent something that we don't have here on this planet. This can be an extremely practical application of space communications.

If you're working on an important project and have problems to solve, explain this to the people you're dealing with and ask for any helpful information they might be able to contribute. Do this just as you would if you were talking to a friend or an associate. Whomever you are communicating with may or may not be able to assist.

In an even more ordinary fashion, they may need information from you about something. No matter where beings are in the Universe, they have the same thing in common. We and they are in the process of life, growing and learning about both ourselves and other things in the world around us. This is really nothing so new or unusual when you think about it.

Remember the stereotyped preconception about contacting wise and advanced beings from another part of the

Universe? Well, the people you're contacting may have the same ideas about you, especially if they are at the same stage of development as we are. After all, they're communicating with advanced beings who have learned to reach out into outer space mentally and consciously, as well.

We're really rather average, normal Earth people; but some of our fellow communicators may not think of US that way. In fact, be suspicious of someone who egotistically claims to be a highly advanced being who is going to give you information to save your world. Chances are that our world is doing just fine, whether we think so or not. It's also not fair to pretend to be the savior for some other people on a different planet. It's not ethical for us to put anyone else on about this, either.

The planets and beings you're likely to run into in this endeavor may be having more serious problems than we are. They may be looking for contact with advanced beings out in space to give them answers to their questions just as frequently as we are. It's a good point to keep in mind. The odds also predict that you will communicate with someone who is not necessarily more intelligent than you, but who does have more access to accumulated knowledge. In that case, just ask about it.

It is not wise to operate this psionic/subatomic machine, or any of the others we're discussing, while under the influence of alcohol or drugs. Your mind/consciousness will have enough to occupy it in its natural state. Likewise, if you don't feel good, are in a depressed mood, or are angry, it's not a good time to be operating any of these devices.

These devices operate with energy generated by the operator's mind, augmented by emotions, feelings, desires, etc. They are amplified, focused, and projected. Self-control is extremely important to their smooth and accurate operation. Every person in the group who is using this communicator should be of harmonious mind with a positive attitude. A practical frame of mind should be developed as operation becomes more familiar to everyone involved.

An expectant attitude is also helpful. What should you expect? You should expect that your knowledge and understanding will grow at a faster rate. You can expect your mental capabilities and talents to increase as you work with expanded concepts and perceptions. Emotional developments can be expected to grow in proportion to strong desires for more understanding of yourself and your Universe.

There are two other effects that the Crystal Communicator can be used to achieve. One is the forcefield effect. When this is in use, it seems to create energy dome circles around itself. (We will look at this further in Chapter 8.) The other effect that is commonly reported is the radiation of heat when the unit is close to people. I have no clear explanation for this, but some people can feel heat by placing their hands over it. Some even see the energy waves radiating from it. This is just a side effect, but it is something interesting to watch for.

Summary

As technology becomes more sophisticated, machines are invented that have no moving parts; the only thing that moves through advanced devices is energy itself. As a society progresses, the most valuable commodity becomes knowledge/information. Even now, over fifty percent of the people working in the United States are involved in processing data/information.

Another occurrence in an advanced society is the increase in the talents and capabilities of the people as individuals. In this area, our society is taking a giant jump in consciousness. We are a part of that process. We are acquiring new knowledge. Regardless of the source, acquiring knowledge is one of the most important endeavors human beings can be engaged in.

The potential for positive effects from these activities is great. The need for solutions, new solutions, to some of our most pressing life problems at this time is also exceedingly evident. The creative actions involved in these activities are also exciting and interesting.

CHAPTER SEVEN

ENERGY OF THE GODS

"There is no energy shortage. There is a severe short-age of creative thinking."

What is the Energy of the Gods? It is the same energy that coordinates and runs the entire Universe, or Universes, depending on your degree of knowledge and information. If that's the case, why not call it the Power of God, in the singular? When it's conceived of as being used by an imaginary being of one God, then it is indeed referred to as the Power of God. When other beings of the Universe, through consciousness and intelligence, begin to use the same power, then that power becomes the Energy of the Gods.

It's been said that in the ancient past beings from outerspace came to this planet and built colonies and bases. In our ancient myths and traditions dating from these times, they were referred to as Gods because they used the creative energy of the Universe and applied it in the every-day world, going about their tasks. This is the state we are in today. We are beginning to apply the power of God through our technology, using it on a routine, everyday basis. For us, the Power of God is again becoming the Energy of the Gods. In this respect, the entire workings of our Universe can be said to be a technology—a higher advanced technology; a more developed and far-reaching technology.

Many of our most successful aspects of the technology currently available came only when we started to duplicate nature, and were a direct result of our learning from nature. There is no doubt about it. The Earth does not have an energy shortage or crisis; the galaxies and star systems do not have any energy shortage or crisis.

There is always enough energy radiation coming in through the star systems in the form of subatomic particles, waves, and fields, interacting with our solar system. The energy is transferred onto our Earth. There is enough energy of this type being generated by the Earth itself which acts as a giant low voltage electrical generator, creating its own particle streams and interacting fields, and from this technology all life derives its energy: plants, animals, people; all work off of this interrelated energy accumulation and flow.

If the entire Universe, right down to our solar system, down to our Earth, works smoothly and continuously, it is only reasonable and logical that we take a closer look at these interrelated, interacting systems. This is the ultimate technology; it is the type of technology we can reproduce because it's derived from a source of energy that is present everywhere, continuously flowing in abundance 24 hours a day, every day. This is the Energy of the Gods.

Who uses the Energy of the Gods? Those who use it, rather than being especially enlightened beings (highly advanced may be a good term to use for them), are more than likely to be people who have evolved through enough stages of trial and error to be frustrated enough that they have begun to look for alternatives to energy and, in the process, have stumbled across the obvious example of nature itself. To add a positive connotation to frustration, I'd call it "creative frustration", rather than the desire to become great, enlightened and knowledgeable. We need to use creative frustration as the motivation to enter into creation and usage of the universal energy which becomes, when used by co-creators and human beings, the ultimate technology.

How hard is it to use the ultimate technology? As we have mentioned before, we really do use universal energy every day. It's the same energy that flows to us from the Earth and the stars. It's the same energy that flows along the nerves in our bodies; the same energy that sends impulses to our brain and that our brain uses to send impulses to our arms and mouths and eyes.

We are already using the ultimate technology, even though it's more in a passive sense of the term. We use it when we breathe; when we walk; when we dream. The time it really becomes ultimate is when we consciously begin to create machines to use it, and increase our total awareness to where we are able to increase the development of our total talents and capabilities. Using the ultimate technology increases spiritual growth, mental growth, emotional growth, and has positive benefits on our physical health.

As an Earth race, we have just reached the point of having a foundation for our future growth in developing our relationship to the universal energy. This is the ultimate technology of the Universe. Wherever we are, this energy comes to, flows through, and around us.

In the next stage of our development, we consciously create and direct our own evolution. We will be learning to use the flow of universal energy in both ways. Instead of sitting back and letting it come into us and do what it will, we will consciously create and project energy and ourselves farther out. How far we go depends on our own choice. We are obviously beginning to use this all around our planet. We are now beginning to project ourselves and look out into the solar system, and into the other star systems through the galaxies. We are starting to remove our self-limitations; to move the limitations further out to the edge of the Universe. Our consciousnesses can now conceive of the edges of the Universe.

It was once thought that the Universe was ever-growing and expanding like we ourselves are; that it didn't have any definite limits; that it was endless. Within the last few years, the concept has reached our minds that the Universe is indeed finite. There is an edge to this Universe.

Along with the concept of a finite Universe comes the realization that there is more than one universe. There are many interdimensional and interpenetrating universes, and there are other universes in what we refer to as the "physical realm" which is around this Universe. Our minds have been able to conceive of the limits and the edge of this Universe. They've also been expanded by realizing the simultaneous existence of all the dimensions within this one and the fact of other universes existing around ours.

At the same time as we've conceived of reaching out to the outer limits of the larger Universe, we have also turned inward to the limits of the smaller universes. We have gone from the world of the atom to the world of the particles, into the micro-universe. We have also reached out to the limits of the micro-universe, from the world of atoms, electrons, protons, psions, and quarks, to the hundreds of different types of particles with their interrelationships and their interaction. They reflect the outer Universe and the larger Universe, exactly as miniature stars and solar systems always moving, always flowing, changing, growing, decaying, disintegrating.

It is really a micro-universe. Again, our minds, our science, and our research have reached the edge. The obvious thing for us to do now is to take what we've learned from this exploration of the larger universe and the micro-universe and use it for practical applications. This has been done to a certain degree, but it is still a frontier area.

We need more people involved in this project. It does not need to be formal research or formal experimentation. Neither does it require huge government grants of billions of dollars. Nor does it require huge budgets from multi-national corporations. It requires only people with a desire to explore it. These people are the new pioneers.

Energy is all around us and inside us. We create and interact with this energy through our thoughts and our minds. We already have constant access to it. All the money in the world could not buy more access to universal energy—the Energy of the Gods—than we have at the present time.

It's been written in many philosophies and religious manuscripts that we are created in the image of God. If so, we are co-creators. We can conceive of the one God and the incredible power that runs all of creation. We are beginning to use this same power. There are many of us; we are becoming the Gods of the energy. That's why we speak of it as the "Energy of the Gods."

Are we the Gods we have so long imagined and sought after? Are we ourselves the ancient ones that we sometimes look up to? And are we the advanced beings of the future when we look forward into time? We may be them. This is a difficult position, at best. Within ourselves, we carry the key. Our own minds and bodies are connected and interrelated intimately with the entire Universe.

We've looked far into the reaches of space and seen the edge of the Universe. We've looked far into the substructure of the subatomic world. We exist in both. Now it is time to look to ourselves. There is literally nowhere else to look.

It is to ourselves that we look for the knowledge and information enabling us to use the Energy of the Gods. It is to ourselves we look in order to find out how to accumulate and store this type of energy. It is up to us to learn how to focus, send, transfer, and manage the interactions that we expect from it. It is with the psionic/subatomic particle/wave/field machines that we've been discussing so far that we are learning how to do this.

In the past there have been myths and traditions regarding human beings who could have used this energy without any machines whatsoever, working miracles, so that when they used the ultimate technology, it appeared as magic before the people.

There is one thing we have to admit to ourselves. We have not reached this point yet. Our world reflects it, with its many problems, flaws, shortages, and crises. If even one of us had reached the point that Jesus Christ had reached, we could do a lot more than we're doing now. We are of two minds about this. One part of our mind usually says, "Well, no, we can't go delving into the secrets of creation and the Universe. We're just people, just human beings." This has been ingrained into us from family, school, church, and government. We have been taught to be ignorant, helpless, and dependent on other groups of people for what we do and what we feel.

The other mind currently becoming dominant says we need to strive to know and experience all we can in our Universe. There's no authority higher than ourselves to give us direction. This is really another part of the super-consciousness of the Universe (The Mind of God).

No one else is better qualified to understand the forces of creation and start using them on an everyday basis than ourselves. There are no real experts in the field. Everyone currently alive was born here in just the same way we were. A few of them have lived more years, and some less. Everyone has the same amount of time to learn about it. There's really no good authority that says we shouldn't learn about this—we shouldn't expand our mind and consciousness to understand these things. In this stage of evolution and growing of the human race, the time has come for a few more people to expand and explore the world around them. There's very little else left to do in this lifetime

In the last two decades there's been a tremendous growth of consciousness and awareness. This indicates that the beginnings were started some years ago. They led to where we're at now. It is up to us to continue growing, exploring, and actively using the creative forces of the Universe so that we might understand them better. In physics, the four forces of creation are considered to be the weak nuclear force, the strong nuclear force, electromagnetism, and gravity.

One of the main goals of physics at this time is to discover the unified theory that ties all of these forces together and understands their interrelationships. This is sometimes spoken of as the fifth unifying force. The search for the fifth force of creation has not yet produced results for some reason. Everyone was looking for one of the four forces, or something similar to the four forces, whether it was weak nuclear, strong nuclear, gravity, or electromagnetism. It wasn't there. It hasn't been found.

What is the fifth force of creation that enables us to understand and use the other four forces? We've been looking for something so hard that we missed the obvious, right in front of our noses. The fifth force of creation is the consciousness of man! It appears in the physical realms of mind and thoughts. It goes a step further as the consciousness of man is the controlling force that unifies the creative forces in our Universe. It is so obvious. Yet it has been missed all these years.

When this type of consciousness is spoken of as being expanded, reaching out into the Universe, it becomes a superconsciousness, a mass consciousness, or the mass unconscious, when you're speaking of tapping the human mind into the main center. That is what scientists have been searching for all of these years. It comes back to the old philosophical saying, "Look within. It is within yourself." The main unifying force, creative force, in the Universe that controls all the other forces, is intelligence and consciousness. In this case, human.

We can speak of consciousness on the scale of the planet Earth itself being a conscious, living being. It grows, changes, and moves around quite frequently. We could carry that a step further and speak of the group of conscious beings which we think of as our solar system. We could take another step out on an expanded scale, looking at the group of conscious beings, the interrelating groups of galaxies and the star clusters, as we move on out into the Universe.

On the ultimate scale of an expanded level of a conscious being, we could take the holistic look at the Universe itself as one conscious, growing, expanding being. As we work our way back down, we would go back from the Universe, to the different galaxies, to the different solar systems and stars, to the different planets, to the different moons. We would go into human beings, animals, plants, the mineral kingdom, and work our way down into the atomic universe made up of atoms and subatomic particles, to the smaller scale of the micro-universe. We would still be looking at individual conscious beings or groups of conscious beings interacting, interrelating, coming into and going out of existence.

No energy is ever lost. It just transforms itself and changes form in the process of creation; in the process of existence itself. It's always moving and growing from one form to another, or decaying and disintegrating into another form. The reality of it is that in the entire conscious, intelligent being of the Universe, from particles and atoms all the way up to galaxies, nothing is ever lost. Energy remains moving with the forces of creation.

On a personal level, what that means is that you and I have been in existence ever since the Universe itself was created. We have always been energy forms whether in the forms of matter with physical bodies, held within magnetic fields that keep us together, or as spirits and soul consciousness; energy forms moving throughout the Universe, occasionally taking up a denser form, going through the different cycles. We've always been here. We are as old as the Universe. We will always exist somewhere, regardless of what form we change into. With all this age and experience, shouldn't we have learned something about how it all works by now?

CHAPTER EIGHT

FORCE FIELDS AND ENERGY SHIELDS

"Of peace, Peace of Mind is the most enduring."

A sensitive psychic in Oregon has just finished setting the quartz and crystal stones of a homemade force field at the four directions of his land. He'll sleep better tonight, knowing that the field will protect him from thought influences, UHF and VHF waves that have been disturbing his peace of mind.

There are several different types of force field and energy shield generators. The first is the Home and Garden Field Projector. Like the others, it is simple and economical to build and use. Often it can be constructed from materials left over from our earlier experiments. Sometimes when purchasing quartz crystals at rock shops, a cluster of crystals is acquired in order to get the main crystals the right size for our projects. The small cluster of crystals can be used for this project, after the larger ones have been removed. The other materials necessary are plain white quartz rocks that can usually be picked up while on a camping trip in the country. They are sometimes found along river beds or around areas where there is road construction.

Quartz is quite common; almost one-third of the Earth is composed of quartz. Sounds vaguely familiar, doesn't it? It seems likely that the Earth uses quartz for dealing with energy in the same way that we do, making use of its natural properties.

Needed for this device are:

Four small clusters of quartz crystals, 1½" to 3" in diameter.

Four white quartz rocks; size can vary, depending on convenience, since they're heavy, but 6" to 8" wide is suitable.

A tube of waterproof caulking compound or sealer for attaching and sealing the clusters to the rocks.

Center the clusters with one on top of each quartz rock and glue into place. To set in place, one should be on each side of your home or garden: one each for north, east, south and west. When these are in place, you may want to mentally project a circle of white light while visualizing a beacon of energy coming from each unit to form an energy dome.

Another way to charge and tune the crystals is by using a Power rod to achieve a psionic/subatomic beam toward each one of them for a short period of time. If these are being used around the garden, they can be preprogrammed to stimulate plant growth and later reprogrammed to ward off harmful insects and similar things, as necessary. At any time, the overall energy field can be intensified by mental and emotional impulses.

An Energy/power Rod can also be used for healing and strengthening individual plants within the garden. In the event that harmful insects arrive at your garden, point the Energy Rod at the entire energy field and ask the insects to leave. Be forceful in your feelings as you do this. Visualize them leaving at the same time. Although it's possible to destroy insects in the same manner, I wouldn't recommend it, since it's just as easy to move them all somewhere else.

Another type of garden force field can be constructed, using small quartz crystals left over from previous experiments. This one can be built by putting the crystals into small copper tubes. These tubes can be from ¼" to ½" in diameter. They should be wrapped with leather the same as miniature Energy Rods, but with the bottom end left

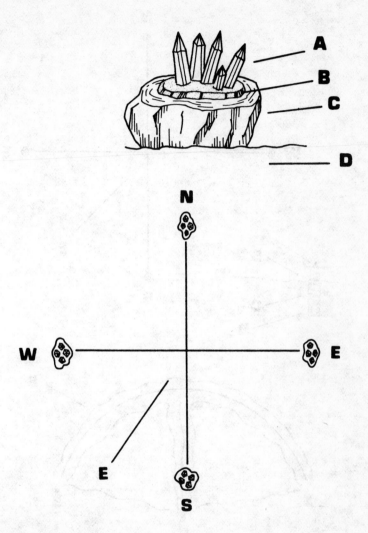

CLUSTER FIELD LAYOUT
- A. Quartz Crystal Cluster
- B. Waterproof Sealer Compound
- C. White Quartz Rock
- D. Ground Contact
- E. Direction - Perimeter Layout

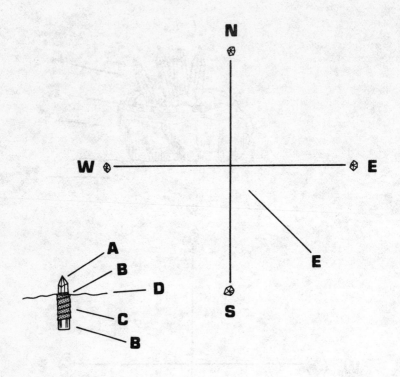

ROD FIELD LAYOUT
- A. Quartz Crystal
- B. Copper Tube
- C. Leather Wrap (spiral insulation)
- D. Ground Contact
- E. Directional Layout
- F. Energy Field Pattern

open. This open end should be placed several inches into the ground. The total length is about six inches, so that three inches can extend above ground, with the crystal on top. Place these at each of the four directions: north, east, south, and west, at the edges of the garden. Four of these are needed, but a fifth one can be centered at the middle of the garden for a symetrical arrangement. White quartz rocks can also be placed around each of the crystal rods to enhance the appearance of the units.

Now is a good time to take another look at the Crystal Communicator device we learned how to build in Chapter 6. This unit also functions as a super shield/force field for house and home. This is a side effect we can make use of when it's not being used as a communication unit.

Not only does this unit make a nice looking crystal display by itself, but it can be mentally programmed to project a blue-white light force field dome over and around your house. After it's set in its place, think of it radiating energy in all directions and visualize the energy dome forming. Charge it with an emotionally strong desire for protection of your home and leave it as such for as long as you want.

What we've been discussing so far may sound like magic. Psionics and subatomics of the ancient and super sciences of advanced beings frequently appear that way. Magic is just another term for a science that is not yet fully understood.

Once before, we briefly mentioned the early psionic machines of the 1940's and 1950's. These primitive devices used some very basic electric parts and wiring. However, when cardboard and paper reproductions of these machines were constructed, they worked as well as the original machines.

The main key to all of these machines is the mind and emotions of the person operating them. There are some secondary factors, aside from the materials; the shapes and patterns do appear to play a part in their operation. Circles appear to be especially significant as they are an important part of nature itself.

At this point, it may be well to remember that there are many patterns of nature that we do not fully understand yet. Like electricity, we can learn to use these quite well without an exact comprehension of them.

Double-Termination Quartz Crystal Energy Shield

A man and a woman walk down the busy street in a large American city. They feel completely safe. Nobody will threaten their safety. In the man's pocket is a special quartz crystal. In the woman's purse is a similar crystal. These are not just any crystals, but rare, double termination crystals tuned to their bodies and biomagnetic fields in order to produce personal force fields of protection. These fields provide protection against mental as well as physical harm. Thought shields of the highest order. No wonder these people feel very secure. Why shouldn't they? They've learned to use the most advanced and oldest technology on earth.

The Personal Force Shield—Biomagnetic Augmentation Field—is an individual amplifier of your own mental forces in whatever degree you are able to utilize and project them. Most people are familiar with the practice of visualizing the white light circle of protection around themselves. There are times when it may be advisable to increase this type of mental shield.

Why would anyone need an augmented blue-white light shield? The main reason is that our present society has advanced to the point where there are too many people and groups of people using psionics and similar machines to influence the thoughts and actions of others. This is a serious infringement on individuals' universal human rights. A responsible, aware, conscious individual simply should not tolerate this type of human rights violation. Attempts at control of other peoples' thoughts and emotions in order to oppress them is not right nor is it ethical or moral.

There are many people who are knowledgeable in the techniques of the Ancients, whether from the days of

Atlantis or elsewhere. They are using these techniques to make war on each other. Whether it's with invisible or visible forces, war is war, and it is extremely offensive. It's never clever when there are so many other people who know what is going on and how to counteract it.

We are, at this time, living in the new days of Atlantis, with all its activities and attendant problems (in a later chapter, we'll deal with this again). This means that individuals may need to protect themselves more than they have in the past. The Double-Termination Crystal Energy Shield is one way of doing this.

How do you build one? Easy; you don't! That's right; we can create one, but that's not exactly the same as building one. In order to do this, one main thing is required: a good quality double-termination quartz crystal. These are sometimes hard to find, but are not impossible to buy or acquire.

What should it look like? This type of quartz crystal should have clear points with unchipped facets. It has a point at each end (or termination). Size can vary from an inch to several inches long. As clear and perfectly formed as can possibly be found will be adequate. Sometimes you may have to acquire several before you find one that feels right for you. Be persistent. Keep asking for them and checking with rock shops.

When you find your double-termination crystal, then you start to create your shield (don't worry, if you have a need for one, you'll find it or attract it to you, or you will be attracted to it). Immediately begin to keep the crystal close to you at all times. Keep it in your pocket, your purse, or at the very least, in your house. When you travel, it should go with you.

A quartz crystal is a transducer and capacitor for energy. It will store and it will change energy from one kind to another. By keeping it close to your body over a period of time, it will tune itself to your conscious and biomagnetic field. Speed this process up by thinking about it and emotionally charging it to the best of your ability. Over

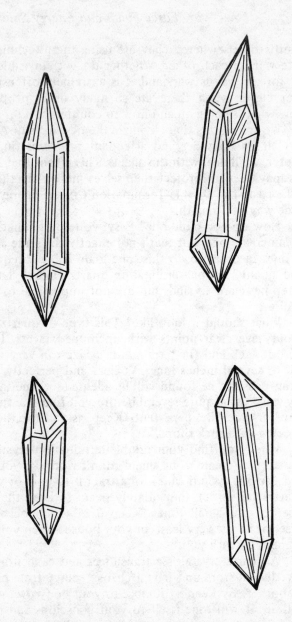

DOUBLE TERMINATION QUARTZ CRYSTALS FOR ENERGY SHIELD - VARIOUS SHAPES

a period of time, this crystal will become fully activated to the point where it will continue to function as a shield even when you're not thinking about it. At times of stress, it can be increased in intensity by your own mental projections and visualizations of the blue-white light circle expanding around you and extending out to greater and greater distances.

This device is very useful if you are engaged in positive actions in our world. It can be a great protection against some of the obnoxious psychic and electromagnetic radiations being used by other people at the present time. This type of shield is especially useful in conjunction with Power Rods and Force Knives. If you've built any of those, you are already acting as a powerful force in the world. I hope this will be a positive and creative force.

Summary

The aging medicine man sits near a campfire in the mountains of the Southwestern United States. Before raising his pipe to the starlit sky, he takes a double-termination quartz crystal from his buckskin pouch and places it on the ground near the fire. Tomorrow he will know the answer to which direction his tribe must migrate in order to find peace and prosperity. The answer from the crystal has always spoken true. He looks at the firelight reflected off his pickup. It's a newer time, but the process is old.

This is a more peaceful use of the double-termination crystal. These shields and force fields will function to the degree of self-control and capabilities of the person operating them. Many individuals are highly developed in this area at the present time. Many remember these from another place and/or time. If you are one of these people, you will be intuitively attracted to these psionic/subatomic machines. That's probably why you're reading this book.

As we've discussed, most of us are familiar with the usual visualization of the basic white light shield. This provides good protection from negative thoughts and emotions, even physical harm, as long as it's being projected. Depending on the strength of projection, it may or may not dissipate as our minds become focused on other activities of everyday life.

The Double-Termination Quartz Crystal Personal Shield can provide automatic 24-hour-a-day service. An unprotected person in an average day is subjected to all types of radiation (from nuclear to electronic) from electrical systems, germ warfare, toxic agents, radio waves, microwaves, solar and stellar radiation, low frequency waves used by governments making war on each nation's people, and much more. We live in a vast sea of radiation of all types and sensitive people sometimes find this disturbing and offensive. This is a useful tool for people who need to not only survive, but to work calmly and undisturbed in helping to heal and balance our Earth Mother and her inhabitants.

CHAPTER NINE

EXCALIBUR REVISITED: THE FORCE KNIFE

"Human beings struggle endlessly; not only do they fight among themselves, they quite frequently fight against themselves."

It is the time of Camelot. King Arthur, sitting astride his warhorse, surveys the valley below in which lies the battlefield of his choosing. In his belt is a scabbard, and in this scabbard the Excalibur with its gleaming crystal at the end of its hilt. He knows he will win the approaching battle. He carries the power of the Ancients at his side, as always.

Far away, another ancient face is looking out across the battlefield. The reflection of candlelight glows in the orb of white crystal. The magician, Merlin, stares intently into a crystal ball mounted on a copper tripod. Hanging from the jeweled belt on his robe is a smaller dagger version of the venerable Excalibur. The crystal in the hilt of his ceremonial dagger reflects the golden glow of light around him as he reaches down beside the copper and crystal tripod on the table to pick up a familiar object. He grasps his wizard's magic wand and points it at the crystal ball. The black leather around the Rod of Power is worn and ancient. Again, the light glints off of the shining copper and crystal. He also knows that the coming battle is won before it starts.

Closer to modern times, a security man at a mining project in the mountains of Idaho is going on duty. After everyone has left for the day, he straps on a survival knife.

This isn't just any combat knife. It's got a copper tube, leather-wrapped, and a clear quartz crystal on the hilt. He feels secure for the long night, knowing that the knife is more powerful than any weapon, man, or beast. He knows it's a miniature subatomic particle beam generator. He is secure in knowing what it is, what it does, and how to use it.

Is it possible to reconstruct an Excalibur-like Force Knife or Sword in our present day? Yes, it is. However, mastering the mind technology required to use it with expertise may take quite a bit of experience and practice. What materials are we going to need for this project? Some are the same parts we used in building the Energy Rods:

A ¾" copper tube, about 8" long (adjust length to fit knife used).

A narrow strip of leather to wrap and insulate the tube and knife handle.

A clear-tipped, unchipped quartz crystal, sized to fit inside the copper tube.

A good quality, dagger-type survival knife of the brand you prefer (preferably with a rounded handle).

To assemble the Force Knife:

1. Cut two 3-to-4 inch slots lengthwise in the tube so that it makes the tightest, smoothest fit possible.

2. Take it off and cut the slots in the other end of the copper pipe to fit the quartz crystal. Insert the crystal for a tight fit and use an instant-bonding glue to bond it to the copper. The crystal is now mounted securely in one end of the copper tube and there are slots in the other end for fitting to the knife handle.

3. Slide the tube onto the handle. If you desire a permanent fit, glue the copper tube to the handle. If you may want to disassemble this later on, just slide it on to fit tightly.

4. Wrap and glue the leather in a spiral from the crystal tip towards the hilt of the knife. The leather should overlap, covering the complete tube and the full

length of the handle. After the glue is set, your Crystal Force Knife is complete.

What to do with it now is a good question. What does it do is an even better one. You have a dagger-type knife with a copper subatomic particle generator and a quartz crystal focuser, or a basic Power Rod, attached to the hilt. Although in the passive mode, the subatomic particle/wave/field is on from the time construction is complete. When this device is picked up by the operator, the passive mode becomes active to a certain degree. The energy field projects from the crystal end, combines with the operator's biomagnetic field or aura, and surrounds both the operator and the implement.

In the moderately active mode, this force field extends around the blade for a few inches. When this field is actively charged by the mental visualizations and emotional desires of the person using it, the aura reaches out far beyond its point. This is the combat mode of the invisible, but very real, world of forces. Except for ceremonial, there are not many uses for this, other than as a weapon for combat in rather serious situations.

Regrettable, but true. That has been its purpose throughout human history. King Arthur realized this device dated back for thousands of years to the times of the Ancients, its purpose always being the same. Unfortunately, in the barbaric days of our modern times, there may even turn out to be a viable need for tools like this again. My responsibility is to relay knowledge and information only. I cannot be responsible for how any of these tools might be used by their individual operators. That is a personal responsibility that goes with the user, as it always has.

In ancient days, many battles were fought and won or lost in dimensions other than the everyday physical realm. Like some of the martial arts still practiced nowadays, the main fight took place with the combatant's spirit or life force. Due to this factor, the battle started long before the opponents reached each other's physical bodies.

FORCE KNIFE

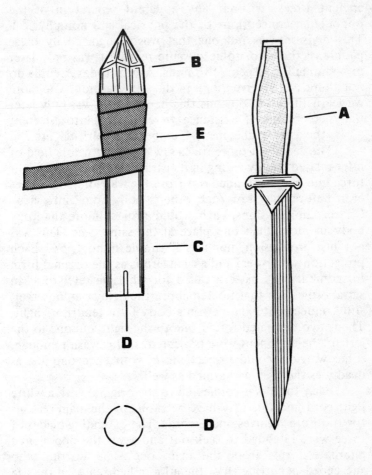

FORCE KNIFE

A. Survival-Type Knife
B. Crystal
C. Copper Tube
D. Long Slots cut for mounting
E. Leather Wrap

Was this psychic warfare in action? It was such in ancient times, without any apparent separation of the opponents' conceptions of the physical and non-physical. This division was not one that was recognized by these people. Perhaps for some obscure reason it was only later programmed into people's minds. As it is today, people do not think or perceive things in the same fashion. The more we learn the more obvious this becomes. It was only later that perceptions of existence were divided into different areas: the astral plane, mental, emotional, spiritual, etc.

The seeing of those times saw only one whole field of inter-related energy acting in its variations. Tendrils of light force lines were extended out from the warriors, sometimes even before they saw each other's body come into view. On certain occasions, each would project more than one body in more than one place at the same time. This was not just an illusion, nor was it simple mind tricks. Each projection was as real and as dangerous as the original form for combat. The pattern called for what we refer to as an astral projection that floated above the field as an observer, still connected to the person's body by a tendril of light. Then, two projected forms, one to the right and one to the left of the opponent were projected. If this wasn't enough, some warriors could project more, with each one just as deadly as the first, and armed as well.

Each form was connected to the original with a white light cord and this may have been one of the main reasons for the Force Knives and Swords. The extending blades of force were intended to seek out and sever the opponent's alternate forms from the main one. The warrior who succeeded in cutting all of them loose had removed the life force from his opponent. All during this time, the warriors would be approaching closer to each other with their bodies and connected tendrils of light swirling together in combat. In one to one combat, this produced a complexity that severely taxed the warriors' consciousness and resources.

What all this adds up to is that we need to realize that

people in other times and places did not think and perceive the way we do today. This may be because our society and educational systems are not made for the purpose of teaching people to think. They do serve their purpose, but creative or deep thinking is not it. We do need to expand and understand our thoughts in order to see in our minds how the Ancients understood the world they lived in. This is proving to be so different from ourselves that it appears almost alien at times.

As a result of their different modes of thought, their technology and science developed in a manner different than ours as well. While they did work with, and build, many machines and buildings out of the materials of what we call the physical world, the main emphasis was on mental human development as the first key to understanding and perception.

Summary
The Force Knife description is a good example to use for recognizing a radically different way of thought. The old saying about putting yourself in the other person's shoes is very true in this case. In order to better understand the Ancients and their technology, try to think as they thought. In order to attempt an understanding of a race of advanced beings somewhere across interstellar space, try to think as they think. This can be a productive but disturbing practice.

In order to better understand ourselves in the future, try to imagine how we will think if we survive and continue to grow in knowledge for another thousand years. When you do this, remember the advances we have made in the last 50 years of this century. Take that and multiply it twenty or fifty or a hundred times. It's definitely something to think about!

CHAPTER TEN

INVISIBLE TRANSITIONS

"Knowledge: It is of greater advantage to know a little that you're sure of, than it is to think you know a lot that you're not too sure about."

Imagine this scenario: a stranger, an alien, has been dropped on a new planet that has over four billion human beings living on it. The basic social mode is barbarian mentality; yet the people have developed a moderate degree of technology.

You are among four billion strangers. In the process of being dropped on the planet, you forgot where you came from, what you were going to do, and how long you'd be here on the new planet. You are an alien in a strange land!

Instead of imagining all this, take a look at how you got here. You arrived by being born on this alien and strange planet. You wonder why you're here and what you're going to do.

According to most science fiction books, a stranger gets dropped on a planet, full-grown, with his phony ID, has to fit in, become average and normal in that society. If we stop to think about it, as we did in the chapter on Superminds, advanced civilizations (certainly further advanced than we are) would have access to all the spiritual technology of the Ancients regarding soul consciousness. An advanced civilization would have available all the genetic engineering processes, an understanding of DNA, and how the soul enters the body and when (while it's still in the womb).

To provide the perfect cover for an alien dropped in a strange land, the advanced civilization would arrange for its own people to be born naturally into that land. That way, there would be no question of authenticity or citizenship. The alien entering the land in such a way would have an exact command of the language, an understanding of the people, of the society, and the ways of its workings. That would be the ideal way to place an alien on another planet in order to obtain knowledge and, as some people have speculated, help advance a whole society at a critical stage of its evolution.

Why would anyone want to help out an entire planet in its development? As a rule, you probably wouldn't care about other people or their development, unless they were related to you; unless ten of thousands of years ago the planet you were working with was a colony of your main civilization. Many of the people on that planet would be your own people, related, just like any other blood-relative, genetically to the colonizing civilization.

This may be the case with the planet Earth. The remnants of the ancient civilizations that reached a high degree of development are here—the pyramids and ancient stoneworks in South America and other countries, remnants of ancient sciences and mind sciences—all the philosophies and traditions passed down over the years, indicate this.

At another time in history, we were influenced directly by another civilization. Many of the people who would have colonized this planet, coming from another star civilization, would be subject to the same rounds of lifetimes and reincarnation as anyone who was native to the planet itself. Many of the colonizers are still here and alive and well today in our present society.

The end result of this would be advancement of the planet, the colony and its people, to where they could take an active and conscious part by rejoining the intergalactic civilizations. They would advance to the stage of trade, communication and travel back and forth throughout the different star systems. This is certainly what we on Earth have been striving for, even with our primitive space program, our space shuttles, our space stations, and our trips to the moon. It appears to be the foremost motivating factor in human consciousness, striving to reach the new frontiers.

Hundreds of years ago the frontier was across the sea; then it was moving westward across the continents; the frontier entered the realm of science. Now the frontier is two-edged. Today's pioneers are striving to understand themselves physically, mentally, and spiritually, and at the same time, by understanding themselves and the world around them well enough to advance into space, are once again taking part in the cycle as human beings are wont to do, of exploring, ever-expanding and colonizing. They are following the same behavior pattern that they have always followed here on Earth . . . always moving and exploring; setting up new settlements; only this time, the same activities take place by going out to the far reaches of space.

Making plans, working toward exploring and traveling in space, we human beings may only be striving and motivated by the desire to return home to the stars from which we came; to trace our roots not just from state to state, or nation to nation, but to the home civilization that carries the same genetic makeup as we do.

Many people regard this civilization as being in the star cluster of the Plieades. This is over 400 light years away and is a cluster of probably over 1200 stars. I'm sure many of them have their attending planets and it would appear that a cluster so large would be the ideal spot for interstellar civilizations and interplanetary travel. If this were the case, the Plieades, the six main visible stars often called the Seven Sisters (one is invisible to the naked eye), appear frequently in our ancient myths and traditions. If they are far more advanced than we are, they may have spread colonies all across the Universe. We might be one of the far colonies that lost contact with the parent civilization.

A great deal of time could pass between the colony's losing contact with its parent civilization and when contact would be reinstituted with communication lines reconnected. In order for the colony and its citizens to reestablish communication with the parent civilization, the people would have to evolve to the stage where their mental development, consciousness, and awareness were able to directly interact with the parent civilization using the same advanced techniques.

Over the years, these techniques were carefully guarded among all the religions and philosophies of the world. These practices are fragments of instruction manuals on mental development, emotional development and spiritual development. They are training guides for retraining and reestablishing a lost contact.

In the later stages of this progression, even if it took 15,000 or 100,000 years to develop and reestablish contact, the colony would begin to communicate and advance rapidly with mind sciences. This has been happening since the beginning of the century.

Our basic technology expands at the rate of almost 500% every seven years. The basic knowledge or accumulated information of our society doubles approximately every four years. This is moving with such speed that some of the government leaders actually say their people are growing so fast, learning so much, that they're losing the ability to keep up with their own people. This applies to business, politics, religion, all human endeavors. We are growing so quickly in all of these fields that barely anyone can keep up with the changes at this accelerated pace of growth.

This explains much of the chaos in our modern world. The old system, be it religious, political, or economic, is breaking down as it becomes inadequate to handle the fast-changing world of growth. At the same time, this is not a doomsday scenario. There are new systems, with new ideas, generated by people creating and instituting new ways of coping with our fast-changing world.

We have both the positive and negative polarities operating currently. One day it may look chaotic and disintegrating; the next day you can see the seeds growing as new forms are created by peoples' minds, themselves, when they're forced to think, whether it be out of creative frustration or just plain striving to make a living or a business success. They are growing as a result of the life process of solving one problem after another.

Living has often been described as a problem-solving, learning process. In our modern times, this process is being accelerated at a tremendous rate, so that every day people are faced with information, knowledge, and the attendant problems thereof. As some of these problems grow, they become critical and have to be solved faster.

The creative frustration again forces us to look further into the inner workings of our physical universe, our mental universe, and we strive to reconnect ourselves physically and mentally with the rest of our Universe and its inhabitants, just to keep up with our self-created growth process. This probably explains why people throughout the ages always keep striving to grow. Anything that's alive is doing one of two things. It is growing and developing or it is disintegrating and decaying, or a combination of the two, simultaneously.

In our society in the United States, We, The People, have achieved (or acquired) most of the luxuries that entitle us to a very high standard of living. One of the few things left to strive for is our own development and that of space. It's one of the goals that makes life interesting and exciting. It acts as a motivation to make life worth living. We also find as we strive to develop ourselves that we keep increasing our standard of living as we go along. Granted, the process does seem slow at times, but it's now taking a pretty big jump.

We are, through self-control as individuals, determining how far and how fast we go. Of course, in other ways, we are also creating self limitations which slow us down at times. As a group of people, nationwide and planet-wide, our mental processes are controlling what's happening on the Earth right now.

To bring it back down to Earth in a more ordinary relationship, take a look at the world economy and our national economy in the United States. Through the media and the connection of television and radio which bring us closer together, we are responding to mental images of an economy going downhill. Everyone thought our economy was going to get worse, and it did.

For some reason of human nature, we like to dwell on it. Sometimes our favorite hobby is suffering; we imagined it would get bad and it did. This was reinforced, recirculated, and recycled through television and other news media. It kept the economy down. It reflects world-wide as well. We're getting tired of this.

So, everybody is imagining that just around the corner, probably next year, things will get better and the economy will improve. We're focusing our minds on the positive side now as a mass consciousness in the world and in the United States, and sure enough, it is slowly improving, and it will continue to do so in spite of change, by going from an industrial society to an information-based society. Our standard of living as a people will improve. The economy will do what we mentally visualize and expect it to do, what we emotionally desire it to do, which is to get healthier and work better for us.

This is a case where every day, unconsciously, without thinking about it, we use the mental techniques that have always been in use by the Ancients and by advanced beings. The one difference is that we're doing so unconsciously, while they are doing it consciously.

When we really expect to see some improvement, as is happening today, large numbers of individuals start to consciously use their own mental, emotional, spiritual capabilities, stand up, and take responsibility for the world we are creating around ourselves. We are always creating and re-creating it with our very thoughts and our very desires. We are becoming more conscious and aware of this, and again taking responsibility. We have the possibility now turning to a probability; we are solving many of our world's problems and we are creating a better world.

There's still going to be some ups and downs in this process, since human nature is self-created.

Sacred Fire

Many of the ancient races had words describing subatomic particles, waves, and fields. Regardless of the language involved, the terms meant the same thing—Sacred Fire. Sacred Fire is an appropriate term to describe the universal forces of creation.

Traditional philosophies mention the four forces of the Universe. Native American religions refer to the four forces as the four directions, or the four winds. Modern physics refers to the four forces also. They go on to describe the four forces:

- the strong nuclear force
- the weak nuclear force
- electromagnetism
- gravity

We have always been in search of the fifth unifying force of the Universe that will unite and connect the four basic forces. While the four forces have been mentioned in religion and secret occult philosophies and knowledge passed down from one generation to another, they've never really explained what they were talking about.

In our times, where religion and physics, or physics and philosophy, cross over to each other, we've come to find that the fifth force was so obvious as to be almost invisible. The fifth force is the consciousness of intelligent beings. That's not to say that this was a secret left out of the ancient mystical philosophies. As a matter of fact, all the ancient religions talk about is developing the fifth force as a key to understanding all the others; as a key to understanding God; as a key to understanding the forces of creation. They talked about human development or spiritual development. Developing personal balance and consciousness. Over and over again, seek the key within. Unlock the door to yourself. This does appear as the main point in the traditional myths and religions that have been handed down to us over the years.

There is a good reason for this. Human development leads to the consciousness that we, as intelligent beings, are the unifying and controlling, self-controlling, force of universal creation. This is not something that has been hidden from us over the years. It is the key to ancient, modern, and advanced science.

It takes an individual who can conceive of the macro-universe with the micro-universe and who can comprehend the inner workings of the Sacred Fire of creation. This symbolic representation includes particles, waves, and fields (which are manifestations of the four creative forces) with the fifth force being a full understanding of conscious self-control.

Why should any individual be interested in this sort of thing? Simply because, by being in existence, we are in a state of constant change as are the total forms of creation and energy we are a part of. For an individual, it is more fun, more exciting, more interesting, than decaying, disintegrating, or dying.

This is what we do by our very nature. It could be termed instinct. It could be termed preprogrammed spiritual growth awareness. It could be a search for personal power. It could be a search for personal understanding. But it is, nonetheless, an innate characteristic of conscious intelligence. On a sublevel, even before intelligence becomes conscious of itself and its inter-relationship with the rest of the world, it is still a motivating instinct. It could be called a super powerful survival instinct.

After a certain amount of time, as individuals evolve and grow, they reach the point where they take responsibility for guiding, programming, predetermining, or choosing with free will, the path their growth will take from that point of their development. This is what we are doing as individuals, as a mass of people, planetwide.

As you can see by watching the evening news, this type of accelerated development on a large scale appears to be chaos, conflict and disorder, and yet, our evolvement forces us to make order out of chaos. We seek harmony through conflict. It forces us to seek the object of our search for enlightenment and understanding, the super-beings which are ourselves. It forces us to take an active part in the purification of the planet and of ourselves by reaching out and interacting with the creative forces of the Universe, the Sacred Fire.

CHAPTER ELEVEN

THROUGH AN INTERDIMENSIONAL DOOR

"If the world is stranger than we can imagine, we should be able to choose the kind of strangeness required for our continued existence."

It has been postulated that there are an unlimited number of dimensions in our Universe, space/time or continuum. While this is possible, our ability to explore them has been severely restricted. Exploration of other realms has been a controversial subject for seekers of knowledge throughout the ages.

Common sense and a healthy scepticism are good characteristics to apply in all of the areas we've discussed so far. Check, double-check and ask for a second opinion from someone with an objective attitude in order to verify the results of experiments to your own satisfaction.

The Interdimensional Door was inspired by many of the Native American log medicine arches; gates of the sun of the South Americans; arches of the Far East; and the stoneworks of the northern tribes of Europe. The Basic Stonehenge shape is one of the easiest to construct. This was an extra-experimental project with results that proved to be extremely variable as well as nebulus. This door can be built on any scale from 6" in height to 6', or even taller. Shape is important and wood is suitable material. Stone can be used, but it is very heavy and difficult to work with.

One of the differences in this project is that once it is constructed, the person who built it has little or no control over what or who comes in and goes out of the door. It is functional as soon as it's set up; it is off as soon as it's taken down or dismantled. This appears to be the main controlling factor.

Although I would advise building a smaller, two-foot high model, the materials necessary for a full-sized door are:

One 4 x 12, 6 feet long.

Two 4 x 12's, 9 feel long (longer if you like to dig deep holes).

Some spike-sized nails (12-inch ones will work).

Upon nailing the lumber together, you have a Stonehenge-type or oriental-style garden gate with an overhang on it. Some favorable results have been obtained by running a copper wire inside the uprights and top from ground to ground. At other times, a strip of aluminum foil (about 3"-6" wide) has been applied to the same inside area and glued or tacked on.

Setting this unit up is a job when it's built full-sized, but the position and process is the same no matter what the replica size is. Finding the right spot is the first step and usually requires some dowsing with a pendulum or dowsing rod to locate an energy center on the Earth that's at a convenient spot. Don't put it in your neighbor's yard unless your neighbor is agreeable and interested in your project.

At the point of the strongest reading, there will be an intersection of geomagnetic lines of force crossing over each other. Sometimes these are referred to as geopathic areas or, in unusual configurations, as gravity anomalies. They are often associated with underground water sources and waterways, since these generate intense energy centers. In esoteric traditions, these have been called places of power and magic spots. Whatever you wish to call them, they are an ideal place to set up an Interdimensional Portal of any size.

If only one portal is being installed, the opening should face east and west. Some rather enthusiastic researchers have set up a square around a circle, using four D-Portals, one facing in each direction (north, south, east, and west). As you can imagine, this is an involved project. One full-sized or smaller model is quite sufficient for starting initial experiments.

What should you watch for after the door is set up? Shimmering waves of energy; visible lights sometimes appear in the air in and around the portal. At times, scenes of another part of the world appear when you're looking through the door. They may be of this world, or of another, more alien world. On other occasions, the scene may be of this world, but in a different period of time, past or future. This type of scene is quite hard to differentiate. As you can see, this extra-experimental project has had results that have been many and varied.

How long should this device be left standing for the first time? This is significant for a number of reasons. Many people have found the actions and reactions surrounding this ancient device to be of a disturbing nature. Therefore, at first, it is not advisable to leave it standing when you're not watching it. We don't know what can come through it from the other side or another dimension. It could be another space in time or another place in this Universe or even another Universe altogether.

This type of experiment is a risk. Curiosity usually overcomes most fears, but it's wise to be very cautious. Spirit beings have been reported in conjunction with the operation of this portal. The most exciting report of using the door was a scene of a super-futuristic city, complete with spacecraft taking off and landing and structures that boggle the mind. Described at the time of viewing were gleaming silver towers and walkways that belong in the realm of science fiction.

This may be one of the reasons many people feel the experiment is well worth any risk that might be incurred. Decide what's best for you, personally, in this particular case.

Some of these portals have been taken down after only a few hours, while others have been left in place for days, weeks, months, and even years. A full Earth cycle of 365 days is a complete pattern of operation since the influences on the portal change with the four seasons. On a shorter scale, a 28-day monthly cycle is plenty of time to observe the strange events that may occur around this area of research. Even three or four days often produce some observations of interesting phenomena. Little else is known about the intricacies of the Interdimensional Portal.

Pendulum Accuracy Frame

A dowser in a desolate area of South Dakota is looking for minerals. For over 20 years, he's been using dowsing rods and a pendulum. Now he's trying something new. He has built a framework that will improve the accuracy of his pendulum. Before, he used the device over a map of the area he was going to explore. Now, he's in the field and after double-checking his readings, he's sure that the mineral deposit is here. When he narrows the location down to a specific area, he'll file a claim.

The next device we'll discuss is designed to increase the accuracy of dowsing readings when a pendulum is used. If you don't have a favorite pendulum to use, it's easy to make a quartz crystal pendulum. This is just a small crystal, about ½" long, with a thin copper strip bent in a "U" shape and attached with an instant-bonding glue. A string 18" in length is then tied to the copper piece. The copper strip should be thin enough to bend to fit the sides of the crystal before it's permanently attached. A solid copper wire can be bent to loop through the strip to tie the string to.

Now that we have the pendulum, what else do we need for this project? Materials needed are:

Four 12" long copper tubes ¼" or 3/8" in diameter.

Two wood squares, cut from a 1" x 8" (pine is fine, but a hardwood can be used, if you want to sand and finish it, and make a nice decorator piece).

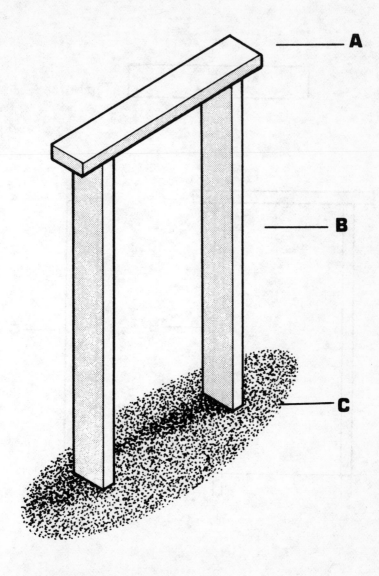

INTERDIMENSIONAL PORTAL
  A. Top Crosspiece
  B. Sides
  C. Ground Contact

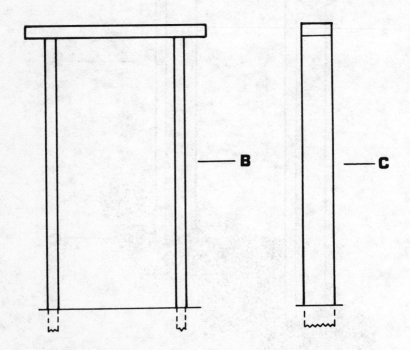

INTERDIMENSIONAL PORTAL
A. Top - Crosspiece View
B. Front View
C. Side View

One small brass or copper rivet (a plug of wood or plastic is okay).

Two squares should be cut, with actual dimensions of ¾"x7" or 8". Refer to the diagram for hole positions. Four holes are drilled, halfway through each wood square on one side of each, near the corners. These should be slightly smaller than the copper tubes for a tight fit.

In the center of the top square, one hole should be drilled all the way through (the other holes you drilled were equal depths and only halfway through). Use a small amount of instant-bonding glue to assemble the frame, but do not use glue when the pendulum string is put through the center hole. The rivet will hold the string in place and can be removed easily for minor adjustments. When the pendulum is in place, the tip of the crystal should be hanging ¼" to ½" above the bottom wood platform.

To operate, place the palm of one hand over the rivet where the pendulum is attached in the center of the top square. Make sure the frame is on a solid stable surface because this is extremely sensitive to movement of any kind. It is also sensitive to air currents. The pendulum will move clockwise for a positive reaction and counterclockwise for a negative answer. Patience is required since the time necessary for the movements is extended considerably as compared to using the pendulum by itself. In spite of the slow operation, accuracy should improve with practice.

Crystal Casting and Reading

An archeologist in a mountainous area of the Northwest is looking for some ancient Indian ruins in a place where they are not supposed to exist. She knows better. She has cast the 12 quartz crystals on the ground. Nine of them pointed in the direction of the ruins, buried far beneath the surface of the Earth. It will only be a matter of time before she makes a major archeological find in an area that's never been opened up before. A smile of satisfaction appears on her face.

This does not use the traditional crystal ball. Instead,

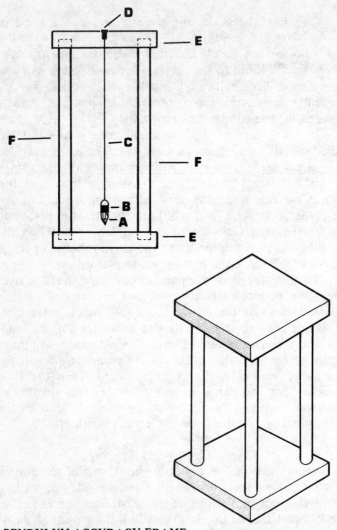

PENDULUM ACCURACY FRAME
- A. Quartz Crystal
- B. Copper Strap and Wire
- C. String
- D. Brass or Copper Rivet
- E. Hardwood Square (top and bottom)
- F. Copper Tube Frame

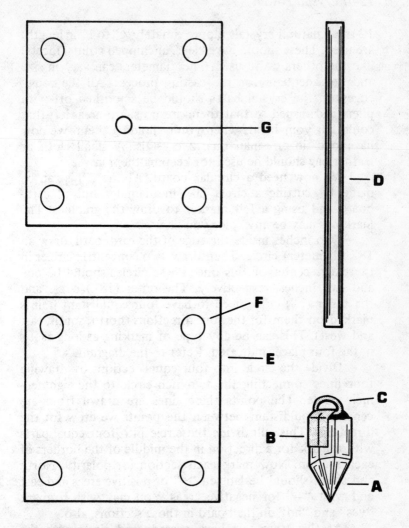

PENDULUM ACCURACY FRAME
   A. Quartz Crystal
   B. Copper Strip (glued-on)
   C. Copper Wire Hanger
   D. Small Copper Tube
   E. Hardwood Square (Pine or other softwoods will do)
   F. Four Corner Holes (Drilled part way through)
   G. Center Hole (Drilled all the way through for rivet)

12 small natural crystals (approximately ½" to 1" in length) are used. These should have clear, unchipped points (facets) like the others we've used. The diameters can vary in size and are adequate for the casting process. All the rough edges on the crystal bases should be smoothed off with pliers and rasped so that there are no sharp areas left that could cut your hands when you're holding them. We now have one dozen small quartz crystals. A small cloth or leather bag should be used for keeping them in.

We now need a circular board. At first, this can be made by cutting a circle 20" in diameter out of cardboard and using a felt marker to draw the graphics. The markings may be any color you like.

Two inches inside the edge of the cardboard, draw an 18" (diameter) circle. Then draw two concentric circles in the exact center of this one. These circles should be one and two inches, respectively. The outer (18") circle and the inner (2") circle need to have four equidistant points marked on them for the four directions (north, south, east and west). This can be any type of marking as long as it's in the four places indicated. Refer to the diagram.

Divide the circle into four equal sections by drawing four lines connecting the two-inch circle to the eighteen-inch circle. The points these lines are drawn from are centered equidistant between the points we drew for the directions. This will divide the circle into four equal parts with a mark for a direction in the middle of the borders of each section. Now mark each section for polarity. North and south should be labeled "+" or positive areas and east and west "−" for negative areas. You may wish to mark "yes" and "no" on the board in those sections, also.

At this stage, we have a cardboard circle with the points of the four directions marked on it and the four equal sections marked with alternating positive and negative (or yes/no) areas. To read the crystals, hold them in your hand for a few minutes until they've absorbed the radiations from your biomagnetic field. Hold your handful of crystals over the center concentric circles, about three

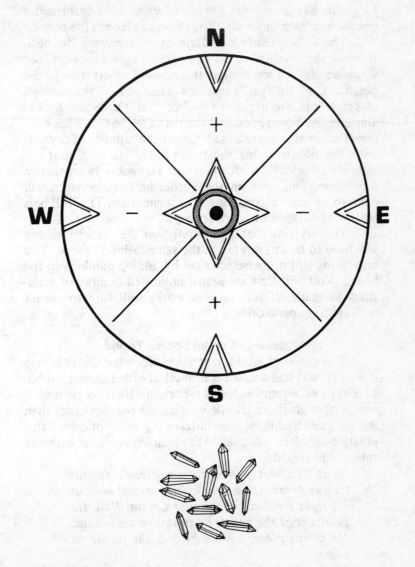

CRYSTAL READING BOARD AND TWELVE QUARTZ CRYSTALS

to six inches above the board. After you have formed a question in your thoughts, drop the crystals onto the board.

The actual reading is done by interpreting the positions of the crystals on the circle. Let's take a look and see what we have. First, count the number of crystals in the positive ("+" or "yes") sections. Then, count the number of crystals in the negative ("−" or "no") sections. By examining the board, you will see that a "+" or "−" for each direction is also represented. Count the number of crystals with the points facing the two positive areas. Count the number of crystals with the points facing the two negative directions. The ones on the border halfway between will have to be read according to the inclination. This will be a matter of judgement on your part.

The crystals that fall exactly on the center bullseye will have to be interpreted in the same fashion as well. You may want to improvise later on by adding numbers to the board. You will find an almost unlimited number of variations available. If this process works well for you, don't hesitate to expand on it.

Atlantean Crystal Sphere Tripod

This piece of equipment is exactly what the title says it is: a crystal ball used in conjunction with a copper tripod. This type of equipment was reportedly used by Nostradamus, although there is little verification for this other than legend and tradition. One interesting description of this practice involves using an Atlantean Power Rod with the sphere and tripod:

As it sits on top of a copper tripod, Nostradamus peers into a clear quartz crystal ball. In his right hand is the familiar Crystal Rod. He points it at the ball as he strains to see within. He is not pleased when he sees the future to come.

First, let's look at the setup of the main unit we'll be examining. This is the traditional crystal ball. The other part is a stand or base built from copper tubing that is ½" to 3/8" in diameter. The tripod of copper tubing can be tied together near the top with solid copper wire or welded, depending on your preference. The contact at the top should be high enough that the crystal ball sits in the triple "V" formed, and slightly over one-half of the sphere is above the top ends of the copper tubes (refer to the diagram).

The size of this project is variable. The 12" tubes are in proportion to a 1" diameter quartz crystal ball. You may want to use a larger sphere (two, three, or four inches in diameter). In this case, increase the length and diameter of the copper pipes.

We now have a finished tripod made of copper. The process is the same as that of a crystal ball set on any other kind of base. Exactly what the copper tripod stand does in relation to the sphere is not clearly understood. The interrelationship between the reader and crystal ball is surely the same as always, but we would assume that the impressions obtained should be quicker and clearer.

For an interesting and little known, aspect of this operation, use an Atlantean Power Rod in combination with the sphere. As Energy Rods are normally used to discharge energy and charge other objects, it would be logical to expect the beam from the rod to intensely charge the crystal ball for more efficient operation or reading.

For another variation of this project, place the entire unit inside a glass pyramid in order to increase the amount of energy in operation. There is virtually nothing known about this type of usage, but it does appear to be an experiment with exciting possibilities.

Summary

The implements described in the previous chapters have been built and used in the United States and abroad since the mid-1970's. We've made a departure from the tried and tested devices earlier to experimental projects and new experiences. The experiments discussed here are part of the process that make it possible for anyone to

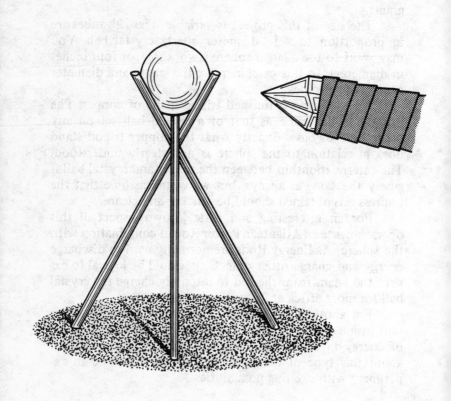

CRYSTAL BALL TRIPOD

participate in the action on the frontier of change. These were included to provide an opportunity for pioneers of the mind to learn about things that we don't understand well enough to describe yet.

This has been the practice with all of the inventions or reinventions we have dealt with so far. Our main accomplishment has been to provide the foundation for future acquisition of knowledge by learning how to construct these items. With the machine or artifact in hand, we have a starting point for learning about ourselves as we learn about the devices and energies involved.

The sharing and communication of newly-gained knowledge with others is a key factor in action. Many times, groups of people decided to work together and assist each other in building and experimenting with this information. This cooperation led to more understanding in a shorter period of time than anyone ever thought possible.

Don't hesitate to talk to and communicate with friends who share the same interests. It's a positive action that consistently produces beneficial results for everyone involved. Any of the items we've described are able to inspire new innovative experiences. The frontier, the sharp edge of change, is wide open territory!

. . . . A Canadian geologist and his friend, an electronics technician, have just completed building a Power Rod and some other quartz crystal devices. They think of great possibilities for the future. If they can do it, they'll build a copper and crystal mining extractor that focuses energy straight into the Earth, locking onto the particles of the precious minerals they hope to extract. This may turn out to be an efficient and environmentally safe method of mining in the future. They're on the frontier of change in their lifetime! . . . .

CHAPTER TWELVE

QUARTZ CRYSTALS

"Whenever we look into the structure of our Universe, the Earth, trace elements in our bodies, even table salt, one form appears as a common denominator: the crystal."

We will attempt to trace the history of crystal information. It has been widely reported that a super-ancient civilization, Mu, existed approximately 60,000-80,000 years ago. There have been civilizations on Earth that predate what we consider ancient. Some of these go back millions of years, but for our purpose we'll start with Mu.

In the time of Mu, Crystal Power Rods were used, Crystal Staffs were in existence, as were what was later to become the Atlantean Crystal Headband. We would assume that these devices were used for the same purposes in the areas of medicine and health as they were later in Atlantis. Obviously, with the positive/negative polarity and the understanding of the healer and warrior, these Energy Healing Rods were also used among the warrior class as weapons of war. Among the ruling classes, these came to be symbols representing the power of the Universe embodied on Earth.

At this point, we'll leave Mu and move on to a time perhaps 12,000-15,000 years ago (a rough estimate) to the civilization of Atlantis. At this time, crystal energy machines formed the main basis of civilization. The healers and doctors used Energy Rods for medical purposes. Soldiers used rods and staffs as their weapons of war. Researchers and scientists used the Crystal Headbands for communicating with people throughout the Universe.

Also at this time, crystals were used to enhance the aura or energy field of the human body, mainly by the soldiers, and to ward off the effects of other soldiers using this same type of energy device. The Shields and Force Fields were in common use.

Other areas of Atlantis have been described as using the giant power crystals in the tops of pyramids to accumulate and focus energy within the form and transmit it to other areas, perhaps running transportation: ground, sea, and air. This has been reported as a source of energy that was transmitted to other buildings to provide light and the basic necessities at that time. We can assume that there were other far-reaching uses of crystal power. However, these others have not been sufficiently verified or re-created.

We will assume that the story of devisive forces in Atlantis which caused its downfall and destruction is true. From civilization, the people of that time descended into barbarism.

The next time we find Power Rods in use is in the time of Moses, more than 2,000 years ago. Generally, the best descriptions were not of the rods themselves, or the staffs. The most vivid descriptions were mentioned in Exodus, a book of the Bible, showing the effects of these Energy Rods and Staffs are used by Moses and Aaron. These effects were dramatic and far-reaching.

At this point there's another gap between the times these devices were in use. From this period we would proceed to the legend, or tradition, of King Arthur and Merlin. Usual references concentrated on the sword, Excalibur, carried by King Arthur. The description of the sword is generally routine, with the exception of the crystal or gem mounted on the end of the handle. This description matches exactly what would be the equivalent of a Force Knife on a larger scale, and would be the magic sword of the time.

There have been vague references to Merlin working

with crystal spheres, and it could be assumed that he was also using, or had access to, the technology of Atlantean Power Rods. Not much more information exists from that time period.

The next point where Atlantean technology is mentioned is with the great prophet, Nostradamus. The technology available to him may explain the accuracy of his prophecies. He was described as using a crystal sphere or crystal ball, with the crystal ball sitting on the apex of a copper tripod. To charge and increase the intensity and interaction of this device, Nostradamus was presumed to be in possession of an Atlantean Power Rod.

As you can see, the search for information or knowledge about Atlantean crystal energy devices throughout history has been sketchy, vague, incomplete, and almost unverifiable in many cases. There were some ancient references to the Far East, to the rainmaking and weather modification abilities of the esoteric groups now called sufis.

There are always references to magicians and wizards with their magic wands and rods of power. We can assume in some cases that these were the authentic Atlantean Power Rods. In other cases, they were only symbolic reproductions and replicas and the people who built or possessed them did not fully know how to work or utilize them. While they were in use for ceremonial occasions, the full knowledge of what they were or how to operate them was lost to most of these wizards and magicians.

In the same vein, the crystal ball has traditionally been considered the main implement of gypsy fortune tellers and psychics through the ages. The image of the crystal ball has become a popular stereotype.

Some people of our modern day consider the quartz crystal to be the main mineral element or energy stone of the age of Aquarius.

Closer to modern times, but before the New Age, some of the South and North American Indians carried quartz crystals in their medicine bags and among their ceremonial objects. A few of the recovered uses that have been handed down by tradition have been learned by people who study esoteric lore.

One main use was that of a large quartz crystal sitting in a circle's center. The group around it would use a process similar to meditation and would pick up communications from spirit beings, or from people who could have been further out in space (telepathy, or simple thought transmission). The same process was used to obtain divine inspiration from the Great Spirit, or the conception of God that the people held in their minds at the time.

Use of the smaller, double-termination crystals in the Southwest was to focus the mindwaves (again telepathy or thought transmission) to send messages across great distances. These messages were sent between the minds of people on the Earth, and across the Earth. One especially interesting process was discovered where the person involved would use the crystal to focus mind waves by beaming them at the Moon during its full period, and rebeaming them back to another person on Earth. In this way, communication between people at different points on the planet took place. This process literally bounced thought transmissions off the Moon after focusing them through a quartz crystal.

Present day uses, other than the electronic technology surrounding us, would be the same as those we are discussing in this book with the addition of a few extras.

The pyramid copper crystal cap, for pyramid-shaped buildings and houses, has been reintroduced. This consists of a six to eight inch copper pyramid with a quartz crystal mounted on the apex, its clear-pointed facets pointing upward. This is a reintroduction of the ancient Egyptians, or the pyramid builders that precede the Egyptians.

Another experimental invention is the Atlantean Crystal Headband, but changed in that the crystal itself is replaced with a cut crystal pyramid mounted on the silver disc. And, lastly, some of the more inventive and naturally human applications of the Atlantean Power Rods, or crystal Energy Rods, have come about when these were combined with the early generation psionic black boxes of the forties and fifties. They are not all in box form any more, although some basic electronic parts are used.

The first one to come into use, or one of the first, was the Subatomic Particle Beam Rifle. It looks like any ordinary rifle stock. Its tubular barrel is combined with a crystal focuser and some basic electronic parts. The trigger has been replaced with an electronic switch.

The other modern application is the Psionic Subatomic Particle Beam Pistol, looking like nothing so much as a Buck Rogers' space gun, which is what it is. This uses the same crystal focuser, some electronic parts, knobs, and switches, and has become popular among certain people. Originally it was called the "Autoelectromag", but it has come to attract other names such as "The Freedom Gun" and "The Justice Gun".

This pistol is the most powerful hand weapon known to man. Its particle beam generator has the capacity to produce a beam of particles that will disrupt and disorient the photons of a laser, cancelling out their effect. It is more powerful and long-range than any laser ever invented.

As this type of invention progresses, like computers or anything else, it has the tendency to become smaller. Therefore, the next invention brought into existence was a smaller version of the Autoelectromag. This is essentially a five-inch long pocket pistol using the same technology, electronic switches, crystal focuser and accumulator.

Along with this came the need for shielding devices. The Aggressive Shield was the next device to be brought into play. It is similar to the Personal Force Field and Shield mentioned earlier, except that this time, the crystal is in a small plastic case, with a switch and fail-safe mechanism in order to arm it, and is used in conjunction with the rifles and pistols of psionic subatomic nature. It's called an Aggressive Shield because of the way it's built. It tends to pick up on harmful influences or intentions, or thoughts, and return these to the sender who is approaching the field, multiplied and amplified ten to a hundred times over. Instead of being a passive shield, it is indeed an aggressive, psionic, subatomic particle shield.

The Crystal By Itself

Quartz crystals (silicon dioxide) act as tranducers, transforming, converting and transmuting energy from one type to another. Quartz crystals also act as capacitors storing energy or building up a charge that can later be discharged. The crystals act as multiwave oscillators. This relates to the transducer application in that it deals with varying frequencies of energy waves, particles, and fields.

In the previous information we've dealt with, the key ingredient has always been the quartz crystal. We'll discuss some of the implied, suspected, or established characteristics of the quartz crystal, itself.

As well as other types of energy, the quartz crystal is said to attract and absorb terrestrial energy of a geomagnetic nature from the Earth's magnetic field. There would also be cosmic energy (solar radiation) that crystals collect and absorb. We should remember that solar energy does not have just one source, our Sun, as it also is emitted in the form of electromagnetic waves, cosmic radiation, and subatomic particles from all the suns that exist in the Universe. Solar energy is available and coming in in the form of cosmic particles and waves at all times.

The quartz crystal is a hexagon, six-sided, usually with a point on one end. The strongest energy points are located at the ends. In a double-termination quartz crystal, there are two pointed ends, both having very strong energy focus points. Broken off of the structure from which it grew, a regular crystal has one base end. This is also a strong energy point, even though it doesn't have the point and facets of the other end.

It's interesting to note that quartz crystals grow deep within the Earth. They usually grow best and clearest in an environment without light, water, or much fresh air. Growing in clusters similar to plants or trees, they do have growth rings or lines on them similar to those of a tree trunk.

A natural quartz crystal, two inches long and three-quarters of an inch in diameter, may take almost ten thousand years to grow. The larger ones we've talked about, the ones that are six inches tall and three inches in diameter, can take up to 50,000 years to grow. They are naturally occurring in the Earth, and it's been estimated that over one-third of the entire Earth's mineral structure is quartz of one form or another. This is true of granite, which is 33 percent quartz.

The Earth has an abundance of quartz crystals and rock as part of its makeup. This naturally-occurring quartz, and the quartz crystals that grow within the Earth, emit an energy field and work in an interaction with the Earth's field. The Earth actually functions as an electromagnetic generator, probably using the naturally-occurring quartz, along with its cosmic and geomagnetic characteristics in combination with the piezoelectric effect. The piezoelectric effect occurs when atoms and molecules of crystals are excited through heat or pressure and produce an electric charge.

The quartz crystal naturally emits an energy field. This field appears with a blue center or a blue-gray inner field and a white outer field, sometimes occurring in shades of yellow. When a quartz crystal is photographed using Kirlian photography equipment, it appears as a blue star with white energy radiating in all directions around a bright blue energy center.

When light is emitted from a quartz crystal, it is generally considered to be blue, passing on into white. Sometimes the light inside a quartz crystal has been observed as miniature star-like forms.

A body in contact with a quartz crystal picks up a charge of energy from the crystal that has been contacted. Any object or body under charge by a crystal can reach its saturation point in only a few minutes—a very short period of time. Greater intensity has been observed after longer periods of exposure.

Energy from crystals passes through and penetrates

all bodies of matter. In relation to water, H_2O, or charging of water, this energy spreads the atomic structure in the water. When an object or water is charged with crystal energy past a point of a few minutes, the excess energy rises as a blue mist. This is observable by some of the more sensitive people. The crystal energy force also occurs in conditions of positive and negative polarity.

Many experiments performed involve equalizing the polarities, or balancing them. Some people believe that the crystalline force is emitted from several things other than quartz crystals. Although only a small part of the crystal energy spectrum, one of the associated crystalline force emitters would be a magnet. Two others considered to emit this force are the human hand and the Sun. These four things are said to be closely related when it comes to crystal energy.

The natural crystal functions as an entity unto itself and grows like a living plant, even though the growth period is thousands of years. The crystal functions in an interrelationship with the planet, mineral and biological elements in the area where it occurs, while absorbing and acting as an energy circuit which interacts with cosmic energy radiating from other solar systems and galaxies. This forms the intimate crystalline connection that is found throughout energy and matter.

The universal form or common denominator is the crystalline form. Most other minerals occurring in nature, when broken down and examined in their microstructure, also exhibit crystalline form. A crystalline structure is as common to other mineral elements as it is to biological bodies indigeneous to this planet. It would be reasonable to assume that from the limited amount of space, inter-solar system activity, and exploration that's taken place so far, the crystalline structure is universal throughout all condensed forms of energy which we normally refer to as matter. Not only is the energy and radiation of particles and waves universal to the creative force of the Universe, but even the structure itself is universal in scope and purpose.

By examining this one key, we can have access to all forms, whether referred to as matter or energy, throughout our Universe.

TIMES OF CHANGE

Speculations on the New Atlantis

CHAPTER THIRTEEN

POTPOURRI

"Only the most powerful people on Earth are strong enough to be understanding."

"The Great Chief in Washington sends word that he wishes to buy our land!

How can you buy or sell the sky, the warmth of the land? Every part of this Earth is sacred to my people. Every shining pine needle, every sandy shore, every mist in the dogwoods, every clearing, and humming insect is holy in the memory and experience of my people. The sap which courses through the tree carries the memories of the Red Man. . .

We know that the White Man does not understand our ways. One portion of land is the same to him as the next, for he is a stranger who comes in the night and takes from the land whatever he needs. The Earth is not his brother, but his enemy, and when he has conquered it, he moves on. He leaves his father' graves behind and he does not care.

He kidnaps the Earth from his children. He treats his mother, the Earth, and his brother, the Sky, as things to be bought, plundered, sold like sheep or bright beads. His appetite will devour the Earth and leave behind only desert.

There is no quiet place in the White Man's cities . . . and what is there to life if a man cannot hear the lonely cry of the whippoorwill or the arguments of the frogs around a pond at night?

The air is precious to the Red Man, for all things share the same breath—the beast, the tree, the man—they all share the same breath.

The White Man must treat the beasts of this land as his brothers . . . I have seen a thousand rotting buffalo on the prairie left by the White Man who shot them from a passing train. I am a savage and I do not understand how the smoking iron horse can be more important than the buffalo that we kill only to stay alive.

What is a man without the beast? If all the beasts were gone, man would die from a great loneliness of spirit, for whatever happens to the beast soon happens to man. All things are connected.

Teach your children what we have taught our children, that the Earth is our mother. Whatever befalls the Earth befalls the sons of the Earth. If men spit upon the ground, they spit upon themselves.

This we know. The Earth does not belong to man; man belongs to the Earth. This we know. All things are connected . . . man did not weave the web of life; he is merely a strand in it. Whatever he does to the web, he does to himself.

Continue to contaminate your bed, and you will one night suffocate in your own waste. But in your perishing, you will shine brightly, fired by the strength of the God who brought you to this land for some special purpose—gave you dominion over the land and over the Red Man.

That destiny is a mystery to us, for we do not understand

when the buffalo are all slaughtered, the wild horses are tamed, the secret corners of the forest—heavy with the scent of many men—and the view of the ripe hills is blotted by talking wires.

Where is the thicket gone? Where is the Eagle gone? And what is it to say goodbye to the swift pony and the hunt? The end of living and the beginning of survival."

Spoken in 1854, this reply from Chief Seattle, leader of the Suquamish Tribe, to the U.S. Government sums up the relationship between Man and Earth much better than I could do here. To this day, it is one of the strongest statements ever made on ecology and the environment.

If this was a serious matter in the 1850's, it is even more so in the 1980's. With the proliferation of nuclear weapons, man poses a serious threat to all other life forms and the planet. Continuation of destructive practices by mankind can no longer be permitted to happen. Not only the threat of nuclear war, but the new threat of space wars enters into the picture as modern atomic weapons are transferred into space, along with laser, particle, microwave, and ELF beams—the Star Wars machinery. This poses the greatest threat to life on Earth since the days of Atlantis or Mu.

What little we have left of the traditions and legends of Atlantis and Mu indicate that this is not the correct course for human history to follow, lest it come to an abrupt halt when the Earth corrects the problem—regardless of mankind's wishes. This situation can get out of hand much further than the Earth, the planet, itself. Ancient legend tells us that at one time there was a planet between Mars and Jupiter. During an interplanetary space war, this planet was literally disintegrated to form what is now the asteroid belt between Mars and Jupiter. Some of the survivors who were in spacecraft during that war fled to Earth.

Even though we've advanced to a larger mass consciousness by landing men on the Moon and traveling into space as a matter of everyday routine, few people stop to think that with the devices in use today—nuclear weapons, laser and particle beams—it is within the realm of possibility to set off a chain reaction that will jump the gap from one planet to another, unbalancing and damaging the entire solar system.

A further expansion of conscious thinking will show that mankind has reached the point in their development where their accidental influence could cause a chain reaction to leap from one solar system to another through the galaxy, upsetting the equilibrium of a far wider area. It is bad enough that mankind has damaged the planet. It is far worse to conceive of a chain reaction that could span the galaxy. Whether we realize it or not, we have progressed far enough toward that ability.

It is something that cannot be allowed to happen. Common sense alone is enough to require that. It has been suspected that we are being watched by other beings who know that with the forces we are dealing with in modern technology, such a disasterous chain reaction is possible. This may explain some of the sightings of spacecraft that are apparently from other parts of the Universe, galaxy, or dimensions within this area of our Universe.

Many of the UFO sightings in and around our space shots and on some of our exploratory probes to other planets and moons of this system may be explained by other concerned citizens of our Universe who do not want the possibility of a nuclear or particle radiation chain reaction spreading out into points in space near their civilizations. It would be reasonable to expect that during the balancing, or rebalancing of the Earth, that outside help from other beings will come into play. We should realize as our consciousness is growing and the world is being connected, that we are one society worldwide. The national boundaries are breaking down as we recognize we are one group of people on one planet, regardless of religion, politics, or economics.

In a wider scheme of things, we should now consider

that we are citizens of the Universe, and our responsibilities lie with the Creator; not with political parties or nations, states or corporations, or religions, but with the Universe, itself. This is a greatly expanded scale and level of consciousness. It is necessary now to take our part as events unfold in order to understand our relationship in a holistic mode.

This is not something to be put off for the future, and it is not something that someone else will be responsible for later on, years from today. It is not years in the future. It is not going to happen in someone else's lifetime. It is here now and must be dealt with responsibly by us in the present, in our lifetime.

Healing Thinking

A good example of different thinking is represented by today's medicine. The medicine of modern times will transplant organs, build artificial body parts and transfer blood from one person to another. Ancient and off-world advanced healing technology, with an understanding of the cell blueprint for the entire body, would not even think of organ transplant or synthetic body parts. Civilized healers would stimulate the biological organism to regenerate or regrow the necessary organs or body parts from the original cell blueprint. This is using the normal, natural process. Your second set of teeth grew in in just that way. Damaged skin and bones repair themselves according to natural laws. The process only differs by the degree of reconstruction and speed of regeneration.

Helping and Healing the Earth Mother

According to the traditions of Native Americans, we are in the time of Earth Purification. This occurs periodically over the scheme of time, measured in tens of thousands of years, and is part of a natural cycle. As you may know, the Earth Mother herself is very sick, or unbalanced. With all the contamination, pollution of water, air, and soil, we see and feel the effects in the form of smog and contaminated water where no fish or plants will grow. There are vast areas of our land where some of our animals and birds are becoming extinct. Contaminated by radiation, nuclear radiation such as alpha, beta, and gamma, there are areas where even man cannot live because of the degree of imbalance on the Earth.

In times like these, the Earth Mother will seek to equalize, balance, and heal herself. This process can be very disturbing with its upheavals to humankind who are not in harmony with The Great Spirit and Earth Mother who created them, supports them, and provides for all their needs. At a time like this in historical passage, there is a choice for each of us to make. The choice is simple. Which side are you on? It's literally deciding for or against the Earth, itself, in favor of life and growth, or supporting death and decay.

Many of the tools of change we've outlined so far are related to the Earth's purification process. Healing Rods can be used to remove cancerous organisms, not only from a human body or an animal brother or sister's body, but from the Earth. Other uses in the purification process involve beaming subatomic particles from the rods to radioactive waste areas to speed up the natural process of alpha, beta, and gamma decay. Instead of these damaging radioactive points staying in place for thousands of years, they can decay, balance and neutralize much faster than normal. This speeds up a natural process that is already working and assisting it.

Other experiments have taken place using Energy Rods to beam particles into contaminated and polluted water and air to remove the contaminating particles. There is a planetwide network of people engaged in these activities on their own. Other devices such as the Crystal Headband for communication enable these people to communicate easier and faster. It also enables communication to take place outside the established manmade system using electronics and telephones. This type of communication would remain effectively functioning during any planetary upheavals from the Earth's attempting to rebalance herself using earthquakes, volcanos, or severe storms. All of these are natural phenomena of an electromagnetic nature that are disturbing to our modern electrical based technology.

These natural healers are established securely enough to remain functioning through anything from natural disasters to manmade disasters such as nuclear weapons being set off, or warring areas. The healers will continue to function independently and freely with no interruption to their work whatsoever.

The ancient traditions speak of the Guardians of the Earth, or Keepers. Many of these people are now doing their part to assist the Earth's purification process. Up until recently, we've always thought of the old prophecies as happening in the future—always pushed on ahead into the future. This is not true anymore. The purification process of the Earth has been going on for some years and will intensify in the next decade. The process should be described in the present tense. It is now a working process, and has expanded to the point where human beings must choose which side they're on: positive or negative; growth or decay.

What is your relationship to the Earth as a conscious being? This may come as a severe blow to your ego, but human beings occupy a degree of relationship to the Earth similar to the relationship mosquitoes and ladybugs have to humans. A ladybug flies up and lands on your arm. You know that it's beneficial to your garden and plants, and you would probably take the ladybug out into the garden and turn it loose. If a mosquito flies up and bites you, you're going to swat it.

In this comparison, human beings could be divided into two classes: the ladybug type who are beneficial, and the mosquitoes who are not. During the Earth purification process, a lot of mosquitoes are going to get swatted. It's become quite routine on the television news to watch an earthquake or other types of electromagnetic disturbances remove human beings by the hundreds, sometimes even the thousands. This passes many people by, they just consider it another routine act of nature. Of course, it's a disaster to humans, but it is part of the purification process of the Earth's healing and balancing itself.

People who choose to side with the Great Spirit and the Earth Mother have vast resources available to support them. The Earth and all other living things greatly outnumber human beings on the planet, even though there are over four billion humans. In relation to this, you can see that even world super power, with its giant bureaucracies and military might, is of little consequence to a conscious, living being the size of the Earth.

Most people don't like to think about this because it is a humbling experience to consider your personal relationship to the Earth, let alone to go a step further and consider your position in relation to the Universe. If you are attuned in harmony with other living beings, it shouldn't be too disturbing to consider that. If you are not in harmony with a living being like the Earth, or a larger being like the solar system (or even larger—the galaxy, or Universe), you're probably going to have serious problems.

I have seen many of the present-day Atlanteans, capable of tremendous personal power, that would dwarf the world leaders who are always in the public spotlight. These powerful new Atlantean people walk among nature. Butterflys fly up to them, land on their arms and shoulders, and squirrels come down from the trees to visit with them. Birds fly in and talk to them; bears and deer come to them with no reservations. Many of nature's creatures have no fear whatsoever of these very powerful people. That seems ironic because some of these people, besides being the greatest healers of all time, are on an opposite polarity by being the greatest warriors of all time in existence here on Earth. Yet, Mother Nature's creatures feel perfectly comfortable and at home with these people.

The Sea of Radiation
The Universe is a constantly changing flux and swirl

of radiation. Subatomic particles, electromagnetic particles of all kinds, are in an eternal flow of creation and disintegration. All of existence is radiation. Matter is radiation condensed and held in form by another field of force, another radiation field.

Recently, the term radiation has been given a negative connotation. It has come to mean something bad. This is only true of a few types of radiation such as the alpha, beta, and gamma decay, termed radioactivity. Most other types of radiation are not only beneficial, but they are integral parts of the universal process of existence. Radiation particles are always traveling through space, time, and the forms of matter as we conceive of them. The electricity in our homes, the waves from our TV and radio sets, all of the enjoyable parts of life are made up of and use the transmission of radiation.

Our deepest inner being, from our consciousness to our mind/brain, with its surrounding auras, fields, and thought-created subatomic particles, is another form of radiation. Our bodies, our condensed matter, energy contained in form for the period of time that serves our purpose here, is made up of radiation.

When we stop and think about it, radiation includes all that exists. Rays or beams of energy and the interacting fields of plants, animals, people, trees, rocks, and the Earth, are all composed of radiation fields. They are all giving off energy in the form of more radiation which interacts with the rest of creation. This is part of the growing process that we're all involved in and composed of. It would be reasonable to say that in radiation, or energy, we live and move and have our being.

Fire and Ice

The Ancients thought of crystals as a form of ice. This is not far from truth. They also thought of subatomic particles/waves/fields as the Sacred Fire or Cosmic Fire. When this Cosmic Fire is condensed into shape and held in a field of force, it manifests as the universal structure, the crystal. Cosmic Fire is transmuted or transformed into Cosmic Ice. This is of the highest order of energy/matter. Further down the scale are the other forms we see, still composed of the subatomic particles of Cosmic Fire, and reproduced on a smaller scale with the crystalline structure of Cosmic Ice.

The energy of the crystal is thought of as blue-white or white. The snowflake crystals of the north have always represented purity of the color white. No wonder quartz crystals have been associated with rainmaking practices and various other weather modification techniques. It seems to be a symbolic representation of the forms of ice and water that we have on the planet, translated into another energy form.

It is not a coincidence that crystals have been associated with weather modification techniques through the ages. The ancient practices of weather influencing are again intimately related to the purification of the Earth Mother. The weather is controlled or operated by subatomic particles and electromagnetic fields. Part of the purification process is actually the natural disasters that mankind has labeled such due to their limited point of view.

The real tragedy is that some human beings, and groups of human beings, have been so out of tune with nature and the Universe, that they carelessly build cities in the wrong place, over pressure points, in earthquake or volcanic areas, or in places where the Earth obviously will tell you ahead of time that she needs to change herself in order to provide healing energy.

The most unfortunate emergency is the disaster of human beings out of harmony with the nature that provided the material and energy for their bodies, minds, foods, luxuries, and all the prosperity they have acquired. Everything we have here came from the abundance of the Earth and Heavens. I think it would be logical that we show some respect for the Earth and our fellow brother and sister creatures who live in the aura of abundance provided by our Earth Mother and Sky Father.

CHAPTER FOURTEEN

THE PEOPLE OF ATLANTIS

*"The true test of importance in what you're doing
is: Will it still be important 100 years from now?
If the answer is "Yes", it's important."*

The legends of Atlantis are filled with descriptions of
miracles and magic. It is reported that the people of Atlantis had magic screens they could look into and see events
that were happening on the other side of the Earth. It is
said they had globes of light that would turn on and off
with just a wave of the hand. Another marvelous invention
was the horseless chariot, described as having white fire
beaming out the front and red fire shooting out the back.

It is thought that the civilization grew so large that
they used ships and boats that cruised trade routes to all
points of the Earth to barter with other nations and colonies. Who could forget the magic silver birds where
people traveled through the skies at very high speeds, going
anywhere they wanted to in the world. And even more, it
is said that in Atlantis the people had spacecraft that could
leave the earth and travel to the Moon or planets. The luxuries were abundant. It is imagined that Atlantis was so
rich that even the average citizen lived in a home with so
many luxuries, furniture, and appliances that used invisible
radiation for their power, that it would rival any other civilization on earth.

It is reported that all homes had hot and cold running

water, which is a luxury that a king of medieval times would have given half of his treasury to obtain. While this is a description of how the people in Atlantis lived, it is a description of how most of us in the United States live today. The magic screens that enable us to see events thousands of miles away are nothing more than our television. Our great and luxurious horseless chariots are really our cars, which at night travel back and forth with white fire shining in front and red fire in the rear.

Our boats and shipping lanes all move trade goods every place in the world; every country there is. Our giant jet airplanes, some passing through supersonic speeds, are criss-crossing the Earth above each and every area. Our spacecraft have gone to the outer planets, sending back pictures to the "magic screens" from different areas of space.

The description of ancient Atlantis and the description of our modern society are very much the same. How did the people of Atlantis live? Apparently, judging from traditions and legends, they lived about like we live today, even to the point of having all the attendant world problems and conflicts amidst a life of luxury and high standard of living.

If we live like the advanced Atlanteans of ancient times, it becomes increasingly obvious that we have brought back these things with us. As in the case of reincarnation, the ancient Atlanteans, from the priests, ruling and warrior classes, to the average citizens, the complete society of Atlanteans, is alive on our earth today.

While it's still possible that the continent of Atlantis itself will rise from the sea, it is quite apparent that the continent of Atlantis has risen from the minds and creative thoughts of the Atlanteans who are alive today. For all practical purposes, Atlantis has risen once again. We came back into bodies and populated the Earth, connected it the world over with networks of communications devices, satellites, TV and radio, using the invisible forces.

Our new Atlantean scientists are dealing with nuclear

forces, subatomic particles, lasers, and psionic machines of all types, working with the creative forces of the Universe. Just as the Atlanteans of old did, we are doing the same thing. The one difference between new and old Atlanteans may be that as we developed this time, more emphasis was put on development of material technology, even though our material technology uses the invisible energies of nature.

During our incarnation in Atlantis, we developed more of the mental, spiritual, and emotional sides of ourselves. The rise and fall of great civilizations and populations of people from the ancient days of Mu to Atlantis is like the waves of the sea. The waves of growth develop to a great society, reach a peak, then degenerate or decay back down again. Atlantis grew, hit a peak, and degenerated back down. From some of the descriptions, the degeneration was rather quick because of the forces being used by the society of the era. This time we are developing, growing and advancing to hit another crest like a wave of the ocean. The difference today is that each time the waves crest (waves of human development on a mass scale), they peak higher than the previous ones.

Today, we have a wave that will reach a higher peak in development. This is partly due to the fact that we have developed material technology to a high degree and are continuing to do so. At the same time, although behind the advance of material technology, we are developing the human mind technology, which when combined with material technology forms a synthesis that will drive us on to a higher crest in the wave of evolution.

The new synthesis of growth, while including material and mental technology as it applies to our economic and scientific systems, has reached the point where we are into genetic research and cloning as were the Ancients of old Atlantis. We have reached the point where we transmute materials in nuclear reactors from one element to another. We are unlocking the secrets of nature, of God, and the Universe, dealing with them on a day-to-day basis.

We are developing so far, so fast, that now we create machines in the image of our own minds: computers, which are able to do more and more in a smaller space. Although it is highly unlikely that we will ever be able to construct a computer that occupies the same space as the human brain, with its ten billion cells, we are approaching this and becoming better at creating machines in the image of our own minds. Some of them will be biological computers with parts that grow and expand in and of themselves.

Another area of new and old Atlantis that we are rapidly approaching is the ability to clone, or create, human beings in our own image. Does that sound familiar? And the Gods created man, or God created man, in his own image.

How far have we advanced or how far are we advancing? Let's take a look at the inventions of our times, of modern Atlanteans, and see how they affected this change. Most inventions are invented by someone in their workshop or laboratory—sometimes 50 or 75 years before they will be in mass production or popular use. The first mechanical theories for the television set came out in the 1880's with their electronic prototypes around 1910-20. They weren't really developed until the 1930's and didn't come into popular use until the 1950's. There's quite a time lag between an invention and the time it's in mass use. In the case of TV, from 1910 to 1950, there's a 40-50 year difference in the time scenario.

The same thing happened to lasers which were invented in the 1960's and only in the 1980's are being developed to a greater degree. Lasers probably won't reach their peak of development until the 1990's.

An earlier invention was the horseless carriage, also developed in the late 1800's (1880's or 90's) that didn't reach its peak until half a century later. When cars were being developed in the early part of this century, it was spoken of with some authority that the human body could certainly never withstand speeds of over 20 miles an hour.

People's reactions to new inventions have always been interesting, to say the least. Everyone thought that the great iron horses, the trains, of the 1800's were impossible inventions. Then, of course, the comment about building ships and boats out of metal was that it was impossible to do since metal is heavier than water and would never float.

When the Wright Brothers were developing their airplane, the authorities and experts proved that the airplane could never exist since everyone knew that a heavier-than-air machine could not fly through the air. The time gap from the development of the airplane in the early 1900's took another half of a century or more before it was in mass use as a common-day form of transportation.

Then, of course, we have the early experts who spoke of travel to the Moon as absolutely impossible, infeasible, and never to be accomplished. From the time of the development of rockets in the 1930's until we went to the Moon was again another 30 to 40 years.

Looking back, we can see that the miracle inventions and conveniences that are in use today were here in one form or another 50 years ago. Based on that comparison, or ratio of time, we can conclude that the fantastic inventions of the year 2025, to the year 2050, already exist in the workshops and laboratories of researchers around the world. That means that the highly advanced futuristic technology which we look forward to is already here.

The effects of reintroducing the psionic and subatomic mind machines of old Atlantis into our fast-advancing new Atlantean technology would be difficult to p predict. The part we can predict is the formation of a new synthesis of the ancient mental technologies with our modern material technologies that will compel us to grow to the peak of this wave of development as a people.

As we develop our capacity for mental and material growth in a creative fashion, the other side of the coin is that we have developed our potential capability for powerful destruction as well. I would hope that from our past experiences in our previous incarnations we will not make the same mistakes in the same way we obviously did before.

As we redevelop our knowledge of the ancient Atlanteans mental technology, we may also apply the wisdom necessary to solve our problems and reduce the potential for mass destruction of our home planet. There is no doubt this would be the wiser, conscious choice to make.

As we have mentioned before, the technology of the next century is already present. What we don't think of as being present are the creative solutions to the problems we have created as side effects of our present material technology. It would be logical to assume that we now have the knowledge and information necessary to solve most of the worldwide problems, two of which are diseases from poverty and starvation.

We have the resources and knowledge necessary to solve most medical problems. Although this technology at present is very expensive, it is interesting to note that some of the newer diagnostic devices, like the cat scan and similar implements developed with electromagnetic fields and readings therefrom, are still large, complex, and expensive.

The ancient Atlanteans had a small device that could be held in the palm of the hand by the patient. It was a barbell-shaped crystal, with a silver cap on each end. The doctor could read the colors of the aura or the biomagnetic field of the patient through the energy transmission of this crystal from the patient and diagnose the disease.

There is little known about this device, except its simple description. Judging from the ancient Atlantean devices we have reconstructed, we can assume that much progress will be made in developing this type of technology in the next few years.

One of the major causes of disease is poverty in many parts of the world, and along with this goes the lack of food and malnutrition. And yet our genetic engineering in relation to plant growth and plant hybrids has reached the point where we now know enough to be capable of feeding the entire world.

We have also reached the point where a majority of people recognize the problems we have. This is usually the first step in solving them. Most people do recognize the seriousness of the threat of nuclear destruction and the threat of toxic waste pollution. They recognize these as top priority items to be solved. On a positive note, we as a society have already taken the first step to solving our problems, whether they're pollution, environmental, nuclear, or energy-related. This has been a reassuring development.

We can conclude that the knowledge and technology to solve energy and pollution problems is already present on line. The part of our society that is lagging far behind is our political and social development. The major reason for not solving some of our more serious problems has been the social/political structure which has not kept pace with the rest of our society.

Institutions, governments and bureaucracies are actually blocking the actions or developments that would solve our most pressing problems. But as we said before, our capacity to provide workable solutions for these is already developed to the point of successful operation. We have the material, mental development and scientific machines. All the components are here. It is not a question of saying we will develop these things over the next 20 years and solve the problems after the year 2000, assuming mankind still lives. It is a fact that we have everything we need to work with at the present time. Therefore, since we are conscious of the problems and we have the resources available, it remains only for us to take a direct action on the serious matters affecting our lives.

Will the reintroduction of ancient Atlantean energy devices make a difference in the modern day Atlantis? Yes, I believe they will. This type of psionic or mind machine inspires people to expand their consciousness and think in larger, holistic terms. These devices reintroduced into our society will make a difference. They should provide the balancing effect necessary by inspiring creative thinking with expanded consciousness. Our materialistic technology has created computers, machines in the image of our own minds, and yet these have placed the thinking process outside the human mind.

Any time thinking is transferred to an outside agent such as machinery, there is a great risk involved. If we continue to create machines to do our thinking for us, we tend to think we are not personally responsible. By reintroducing Atlantean machines that motivate us to think and see more clearly, and expand our awareness of the world around us, we will balance the effect of transferring responsibility to technology. For with the ancient Atlantean devices, responsibility was clearly placed upon the individual operator of the machine. No outside responsibility was placed upon the machine itself.

This understanding of personal responsibility was carried over into all areas of life. The same type of energy was used for healing, communication and as a power source; an understanding of the One Source led to the expanded conception of the human interrelationship with fellow beings in nature, as well. While we have spoken so far of technology and ancient machines, we have said little about what was carried over from this understanding into the realm of social, economic and political life.

The best example I can think of for the transfer of this individual responsibility into the social governmental area of society was in a colony or a civilization that either existed at the time of Atlantis or was still growing shortly thereafter in South America. It's interesting to note that in this civilization the government, or the public servants, were very much responsible for carrying out their duties and service to the population they worked with, their fellow citizens.

The difference between these public servants and the ones we have now is very great. These early government employees and public servants sought to actually serve their fellow man, to provide a real service. They did not dress differently or live in a lifestyle surpassing their fellow citizens, although they had a high standard of living and were quite comfortable. The ethics and morals of the period were expressed by the fact that any individual public servant who embezzled public funds, stole, or mistreated the citizens in his or her area, was considered so serious an offender that the punishment for this wayward public servant was to go jump off a cliff.

Now this was a very radical solution, especially if the public servant didn't really steal anything from the people or mistreat them, but simply failed to provide the service of making sure there was food, housing, sanitation or whatever else was needed. The punishment according to the ethics of the time was exactly the same for failure to live up to individual responsibilities as it was for theft.

The other interesting fact to note is that in this society where the ethics were that strong, supposedly not one single public servant was ever required to jump off that cliff. Now that is remarkable.

If, in our present society with its morals and ethics, all the government employees or public servants who stole from their fellow citizens or failed to provide the service they were being paid for were required to jump off a cliff, we would have a mass sanitation problem that would be very difficult to deal with. But this does show the practice of individual responsibility on a large scale in social action.

It can only be hoped that the reintroduction of ancient/future understanding into our modern society will bring about the solutions to many of our most pressing problems by inspiring creative thinking with ethical actions. This should add new respect in the area of social relationships, of how people treat their brothers and sisters. At this point in our society, anything, any action that anyone could express from their own understanding, would be a big improvement in today's situation. The time of just talking about it is over. The time for direct action has arrived.

CHAPTER FIFTEEN

WHAT IF . . .

"Knowledge is power."

Here we ask the key question that spurs the imagination into a realm of science fiction fantasy: What if?

What if:
- in our modern society with all its problems of crime, violence, and threat of nuclear war, tools of change were introduced?
- quick energy tools of the Ancients were reintroduced into our society with all its modern technology and life-in-the-fast-lane standard of living?
- the average individual, who knows the difference between right and wrong, gained access to the Atlantean Power Rod?

Would the average American worker wish to reach out and influence the world around him or her, as the case may be?

If this mythical, average, American held an Atlantean Energy Rod in hand, could aim a beam of thought-induced, thought-controlled, subatomic particles at the world powers considered to be responsible for many of the major problems facing the world, then this person would change the world.

In earlier chapters we mentioned that beams of particles can travel through any material known to man. These same particles can travel any distance at almost the speed of light, some even faster than light. This means that any individual who wanted to focus energy into a beam from an Atlantean Power Rod could reach out and influence world events directly.

A construction worker could aim a Power Rod at a picture on his color TV set. The beam of particles would travel into the TV set, and blending with the microwave radiation and UHF waves which are also particles, ride these as a carrier wave up through the atmosphere into the satellite transmission station, into the source or target. More direct approaches from just one image are also possible. This means that any individual could send a beam of particles anywhere in the world instantly.

In the truest sense of the word, this would be the manifestation of instant karma. Many people in our society have lived their whole lives, for decades, under the threat of nuclear annihilation and extinction. It makes little difference whether the threat comes from a super power thousands of miles away, or from an armed robber five feet away. The threat to life and well being is exactly the same, and this is offensive, unethical, intolerable behavior for human beings.

Any world authority, regardless of wealth, position, or political and military power is now responsible to the other people living on this planet. As it becomes more widely known that the Atlantean tools of the priesthood are back in the hands of reincarnated Atlanteans on this planet, the tables will turn. Any individual responsible enough to take action can now affect instant change throughout the world.

What if an individual reaches out with a beam of energy and disarms nuclear warheads before they are fired? Not only that, can you imagine what would happen if enough individuals had the tools of change capable of accomplishing this when a nuclear war was started? Any nuclear missiles fired could be disarmed in the air before hitting their targets, with only a minimum of damage as they crashed. No nuclear explosions. No threats to the lives of innocent people who wish to live in peace.

Instant karma could change the nature of life on this planet. Imagine this scene: A robber breaks into a home and steals something. Wherever he touches something he leaves a fingerprint. Not just a normal fingerprint, but the electromagnetic impression of his aura. The homeowner with an Energy Rod could send a beam of particles homing onto this imprint affecting the robber's health, his luck, his style of living, or even causing his life force to be withdrawn completely.

The same method could be applied to individuals who committed murder, or any other of the hideous crimes so common in our degenerated society. Imagine the effect of instant karma in the world today. There would be literally no place for anyone committing crimes against others to run and hide; no escape whatsoever would be possible.

So far, we've talked of the obvious imbalances, the threat of nuclear war, and the threat of violence. But our world has changed a great deal in this century and many of the greatest infringements on human liberty and freedom come from the governments' economic system using money or credit, the stored energy of the working people. No government, no organization of world bankers, has the right to use economics to control or force prosperous people (like middle class Americans) down into poverty, so that they can be manipulated and controlled. The process is the same whether you call it economic control, tyranny, or oppression.

Most people know exactly what is right and what is wrong. They seek only a chance to express and act upon what they believe to be right. What if individuals in the United States, or the world over for that matter, could correct what they conceive to be wrong with our world. Would people then take a positive action?

Is this war or is this healing? In many forms of medicine and healing, removal of diseased cells is required. It is required that cancerous cells be removed in order to balance and heal bodies. This is as true for man's society on the Earth as it is for a biological body. Cancerous forms, whether they be groups or organizations, military bodies or dictatorships, or secret societies of economic power people, must be removed in order to balance our society of people on Earth.

Poverty, disease, hunger, war, crime, violence; all of these need to be removed. They are the cancer of the mass consciousness of all of the inhabitants on the planet Earth.

We have spoken of imagining what effects would come about by using one Atlantean device, the Power Rod, after its reintroduction into our society. What if many sophisticated devices of different types were reintroduced into our society? What if enough citizens learned to use the Atlantean Headband to be able to seek out and obtain knowledge of what was happening in their world and exactly who was doing what and where at any given time? What would they say if they saw all of it as it was happening?

The greatest organizations of oppressive people would be totally helpless to exercise their power, control and deceitful manipulation on the average citizen of the countries of the Earth. Is this the beginning of the end? Yes, it is. It's the beginning of the end, not of the world, but of the system as we know it.

The average American is just waiting for his or her chance to do something about it. The effects of the high energy tools of change being used by individuals is chaotic and frightening to imagine. Yet, out of chaos comes the creation of a new world which is better suited to the ideals that most people carry in their minds and hearts. Most people do respect honesty, fair play, justice and all of the higher ideals as expressed in so many religions, philosophies, and political documents.

These high ideals can be manifested when enough individuals feel that they have the power to express themselves freely about what they really value above all. People already know what is right, what is wrong, and just want a chance to act upon their values in a correct fashion.

What if? What if all this was happening right now? It

is. Now is the time.

People, with their families, know they are being taxed out of existence; they are being monopolized and stolen from by giant institutions; they are being oppressed by multinational networks which operate only out of greed and lust for power. Many American families years ago thought they could get away from it all by moving to the country, being part of the back to nature movement. This proved to be false. There is no way to run and hide from the government computers, the tax collectors, the satellites with infrared sensors, the international banking computers with their code and social security numbers filed away; no place to run and hide or escape.

On the other side of the coin, the reverse is true. If individuals have the tools of the Ancients, then there is nowhere for unjust tyrants and power-crazed politicians to run and hide to escape the justice of the people who wish to express it. That's a different picture all together. That's the picture most people have been hoping for a chance to see. Responsible, ethical, moral people would love to express themselves with positive actions to create a better world to live in. They would love to reach out and connect with the powers that be, face to face, in a responsible manner.

The old American Indian saying that ". . . on the White Man's talking leaves there are many laws, but no justice . . . " has never been truer than it is today. Justice comes from the mind and the heart; it does not come from Congressional Records, law books, or speeches. Can you imagine our society as the advanced technologies grow in usage?

Anyone who watches television news is aware of this. They see a world gone mad with insanity perpetrated against innocent individuals who would like nothing more than to mind their own business. But some people have been greedy far beyond monetary gain. The people of the forces of darkness seek to control and enslave their brothers and sisters through any means possible, whether military, economic, political, or religious.

The story sounds familiar already. The people of light versus the people of darkness. The Universal struggle of existence is again being played out on the planet Earth. What if there were enough people with the knowledge and tools to have an instantaneous, direct effect on the events that are important to their lives? Do you think people would act as brothers and sisters and right the wrongs that have been perpetrated for so long? I believe they would.

I believe it because I've talked to so many people—good people from every part of life. These individuals are the ones who make a difference. They are really important. They do not seek to control anyone else. They only wish for the freedom, the liberty to live their lives in peace and prosperity. They would have been perfectly satisfied with that, but the powers that be, the people of the forces of darkness, would not leave the decent people of this world alone to live their lives in the ways of peace and prosperity.

At this stage of our history, the critical turning point has been reached. What if everyone really did stand up to be counted? Many people are making the choice today about which side of the struggle they wish to be on: right or wrong; light or darkness; justice or injustice; life or death; good or bad; and the question is being clearly defined in the minds of those exerting the effort of taking responsibility to think about it and decide for themselves.

What if the ancient magicians and wizards (like King Arthur and Merlin) returned to the Earth in this time period? What would they think of the style of living we have now? What if the ancient priesthood of Atlantis, also divided between light and dark, returned to Earth at this time to continue the revolutionary struggle of mankind?

They have returned. They are here. Over four billion human beings are incarnated on this planet to decide the question of continued existence and growth, or decay and death to extinction. The responsibility for the world we live in is an individual one. This responsibility does not belong to organized religions, to governments, it does not belong to world bankers or economic powers; the responsibility for this world belongs to each and everyone of us, as the sons and daughters of God, as we conceive of it. What are all of these people going to do when they realize the responsibility for this world rests with them?

As you can see from this scenario, the high energy power tools of advanced civilizations combined with the free thinking of people who have a full knowledge of right and wrong, are going to have the biggest impact ever on our modern society. In this action, there are no neutral observers or innocent bystanders involved. Everyone who is alive here on Earth today is involved intimately in what is going on in our world.

Everyone will have to make a personal, individual choice of what to do in the situation of life as we have created it for ourselves on this planet. At this time, it is probably wise to have a workable knowledge of the universal forces that we exist in, around, and through.

What if . . . again? What are people going to do when they have the magic wands of power in their own hands once again? This is a random variable that few can predict. While there are psychics and prophets who predict what's going to be happening, all of it is subject to change from the energy variations involved. The great warriors and healers that live in the minds and hearts of the people, the superheroes, mythological or real, are coming alive to walk the Earth once again. It's a different context to think of superheroes coming from the average, middle class, working man or woman, but this is indeed where the superheroes of today are. There is no way to completely imagine what will happen next. I can assure you that as we wake up to our own individual responsibilities, the changes we effect and create will not lead to a boring time.

Imagine a thousand Robin Hoods. Imagine a thousand Lone Rangers. Imagine a thousand Supermen. Imagine a thousand Wonderwomen. Now imagine a million of them, arising from the ashes of chaos like the Phoenix. In your wildest visions, can you predict the effect this will have on our society, on our world, our environment, our religious, political or economic systems? Will there arise a hundred thousand new Moseses to lead their people to safety and security? Will there arise a thousand new Jesus Christs to go about healing people, relieving suffering and pain of disease, sending out love and kindness wherever they go? Or, in the vein of instant karma, will the returned Christ come this time with a terrible swift sword that cuts both ways?

Let your imagination answer the question for you. No one else can answer with authority.

CHAPTER SIXTEEN

PROPHECY NOW

"Injustice leads to violence. If you want peace,
seek justice first; justice leads to peace."

In the prophecies of the Bible, it is spoken of as
Judgment Day, or a time of judgment. In the biblical reference, judgment means justice. These are the right actions
that lead to and precede, or provide the preparations for,
the millennium—a thousand years of peace, beauty and
perfection. Some ancient traditions speak of a Christ-like
figure who traveled throughout the Americas teaching the
inhabitants of these continents. This parallels the teachings
of Christ in the East at about that same time.

It is interesting to note that the Christian prophecies
describe a time of chaos and transition which sometimes is
called the End of the World, the End Times, or the Judgment Day. To many people, the end of the world means
the end of the systems we use now: our energy, political,
religious, economic systems, etc. To a large number of
people having these things taken away would be the end of
their world. But this is not the end of the Earth. It is merely
the end of some manmade, artificial systems that we are
using currently.

The Native American prophecies speak of the time of
The Great Purification when the Earth Mother will heal
and balance herself. The Great Spirit will interact with
people. This will remove the flawed, obsolete systems that

171

are in use today. This period is a time of disasters and doomsday, with a great weeping and wailing (which no doubt it could be). During the chaotic times described in the prophecies as directly preceding this period, there are a great number of people working to bring this experience about. In speaking of justice, or judgment, it's interesting to note that God's truth and justice will be expressed in power.

Attempts have been made in the last 2,000 years to speak of these principles in words, talk and preaching. There may be some doubt as to the beneficial effects of all this. Has it actually helped create a better world? There is one thing it has done and that is to prepare the way for God's children, as brothers and sisters, to express directly the eternal truth in power.

This may all seem miraculous and supernatural, especially in the superstitious terms we've come to associate with these traditions; but, in effect, present-day preparations are being made just as there is every time a critical point in the history of people on Earth occurs.

Let's take a look at the millennium, a thousand years of peace, prosperity, beauty, honesty and perfection, and all its high ideals and spiritual values that we are in the process of expressing. While there's little doubt that it's necessary for people to learn to deal with each other as brothers and sisters, love one another and care for each other, there are other aspects of life that also have to be dealt with simultaneously and the preparations that precede this time are extremely important.

Far from being supernatural, these aspects of the preparation are very common, down-to-earth considerations. For instance, after the chaotic times of transition with the end of many systems we use now, how will these new systems work and who is going to install them? At the beginning of the millennium, we will assume that people who are still alive are getting along well as friends and neighbors, and expressing the highest ideals socially; but what kind of energy systems will light and heat their houses? What kind of energy systems will provide for their transportation? What kind of systems will be in effect for medical practice and technology, or manufacturing and construction?

In this respect, we can deal with it in some easily understood terms. With the second coming of Christ, we have a new manager for the State of Human Affairs on the Planet Earth; the Earth will be under new management. How are the rest of the systems going to be installed? Can we bring in outside contractors to set up all the devices and machines that will be in use to provide a healthy, happy lifestyle during this millennium?

Since we are currently in the period before judgment, justice, or purification, many of the contractors, mechanics, and technicians are working on it. There are all types of researchers and workers inventing and reinventing the advanced technology of the future to provide for construction facilities and energy sources that are more efficient and economically feasible, so that people will be able to live in comfort and happiness. There are people on advanced forms of energy and transportation, so that we can continue to have a high standard of living, without the negative and disasterous side effects of pollution, toxic waste and economic considerations.

All of these aspects have to be prepared for and constructed as a basic foundation of life for the millennium of 1,000 years of peace. Rather than being a very dramatic, miraculous event, this is a time period we're preparing for by working diligently to take care of smaller, but necessary, details in creating the lifestyle required.

As you might imagine, as in any other major construction project, this requires a great many workers, designers, planners, and creative thinkers, to come up with the alternatives for providing us with workable lifestyles and the installation of new systems to be used during these times. Who are these workers? They are composed of people who are the average, middle class, everyday workers of today. They have just gone one step further in understanding and learning the skills needed for more advanced jobs.

While it would be very pleasant to think that one man, Jesus Christ, is going to appear in public and, with a wave of his hand, transform everything on Earth in an instant. In most religions, Christ's helpers and angels, and various other support personnel who work with or for Christ, are spoken of. This is nothing out of the ordinary, since it merely means there are a lot of new workers who have transferred their employment to the new Manager of Earth.

I think in a great many ways it would help us to begin by thinking of this time period in modern terms. Some of the biblical traditions speak of Jesus turning water into wine. This would denote a person who had an understanding of physics and astrophysics and knew that atomic structure can be transmuted at a subatomic particle level for conversion of water into wine. It would also denote that the person involved had a great understanding of the natural processes of Earth, since nature herself converts the water into wine through rain to make the plants grow the grapevines and then the grapes' natural process of fermentation as it converts into wine.

A man who understood these things 2,000 years ago and knew the working of subatomic physics and psionics would appear as a miracle worker and healer, although he was a humble one who did say that other people would gain understanding. He even went on to say that others would do even greater things than he did.

Other reports and uncovered information of Jesus spoke of him as owning two houses in two different cities and paying his taxes so that his family would have a place to live. They spoke of him as making sure there was money coming in so that his family would be able to afford food and clothes. These reports indicate a very good business manager, among other things.

It's only reasonable to expect that in these times a man like this might return to Earth and would have quite a number of other people working with him in order to effect the large scale changes that have been predicted in traditional prophecies. It's also logical to assume that this would be quite a feat of management and organization, requiring a very understanding person to coordinate and bring it about. There is no doubt that this would require a great many support personnel for an operation or project of this size. Many of them will be people from the local regions as is usually the case when a large organization comes in to do a particular project.

Now we'll go to the other side of the coin in the prophecies, switching from the positive to negative polarity. It appears that thousands of years ago, there was another planetary manager responsible for Earth and its inhabitants. This person was another angel of light known as Lucifer. If he was another angel of light, working for God, he must have gotten off on the wrong track. As is the case when any other manager allows for fallen productivity, poor quality products, inadequate working conditions, hazards and diseases to the workers, and embezzlement of power and funds from the organization, the manager will find himself out of a job. As I understand it, this was the case. Lucifer escaped, was driven to Earth, and beaten back by the Archangel Michael. Apparently he has resided here in seclusion and is blamed for many of the problems and misunderstandings we have on Earth in the present day.

However, as he is aware that the Earth is due to come under new management in the near future, he is probably holding organizational meetings with all of his top executives and managers. So herein we have a part of the prophecy which says a man of great power will arise on Earth able to do many of the things Christ did and fake people out. This man will also be called "The Beast".

In the past it has been very hard to understand how one man could have that much power over the Earth. With our modern news media and electronic connections through satellites and our worldwide network of computers, it becomes a little clearer how a powerful tyrant like "The Beast" could assume this role. The only thing missing from the scenario would be a way to reach out through this network and be able to touch, effect, and control all the other people on Earth. This has recently become clearly possible with the new combination of computers and psionic machines. With just a photograph or sample placed in a chamber, the machine can send out waves similar to those of a radio and effect the emotional, mental, even the physical health of people. It's been said in the end times that this will be possible. Computers that respond to thoughts are here now.

Not having a picture of everybody or samples of some of their personal effects, the only other way to keep track of everyone would be to issue them all a little plastic card with numbers on it—i.e. your social security card, or charge card, where accounts are being conducted to standardize these numbers within a network of computers used to keep track of them. Later on, it has been said, "The Beast" may want to tattoo your number on your forehead or arm with a laser.

A lot of people are not going to take too kindly to this experience. Nonetheless, it is now within the realm of technological probability that these new hybrid psionic computer machines can be brought on line during the end times so that computerized control can reach out, locate, and affect people's thoughts, feelings, and health from a distance. This type of machine also is fully capable of executing people at a distance.

This does explain, however horrible it may be, how it would be possible for "The Beast" or "No. 666" to arise during a time of chaos on the Planet Earth today. We can see now that the conditions for the end time prophecies have already come about. The side effects of them from some of the old scriptures, in a few of the words, . . . you shall not be able to buy nor sell nor get food or clothing without the mark of the beast; people will want to die, but they cannot escape; they will be healed instantaneously and not allowed to escape even by death. The beast will demand that everyone in the world bow down to him and worship him, because of his great amount of personal power and control over people, and they will not be able to do otherwise.

Psionic computer crossbreeds explain the type of technological network that would be in use during these chaotic times of tribulation and purification. Basic understanding of the methods being employed to bring about the prophecies and purification is within reach of everyone who takes the time to do a little basic study. While we have explained the technology of our day that can bring about these things, we should mention some of the technology that was used in an earlier part of the unfolding of this process.

Some years ago, an aerospace engineer studied the part of the Bible in which Ezekiel described the meeting with what was then considered a miraculous being. After carefully examining the description, there were drawings made up which showed that the wheel of Ezekiel was indeed some kind of aircraft or spacecraft. It was redesigned in detail and shown to be exactly in agreement with the knowledge we have today as being workable.

Another case of ancient technology was the Arc of the Covenant, which in the Biblical description appeared to generate high voltage, with radiation as a side effect. There was a portrayal of a person being struck dead by it. This would correspond to someone who stuck their hand into a high-voltage electric box or a small nuclear reactor.

At one university in the United States, the students reconstructed the Arc of the Covenant, complete with its materials which included insulation and several layers of metal. While they may not have completely constructed it, it appears that this was not only a machine that generated high voltages, but it was a machine that was used to talk back and forth to God (so to speak) or their conception of God at the time. It was a communication device, probably very similar to a radio, with other features as well.

We've described the ancient technological reconstruction of the rods and staffs of Moses and Aaron in this book.

Upon reconstruction, these were found to be subatomic particle generators which acted as a funnel for already moving subatomic particles. They were psionically controlled, or mind controlled, and again, this is in agreement with the knowledge of today.

There have been numerous references to spacecraft and aircraft in the Bible. These references are also in legends from Alaskan Indians to South American Indians; the traditions of the Far East, India and China; in short, these descriptions of spacecraft and aircraft appear throughout the legends of history. I'm sure several thousand years ago this appeared to be the power of the Gods coming down from the Heavens, since nobody at that time understood that the Heavens were space.

In our world of today, it's commonplace to see our spacecraft take off and land; it's commonplace to see television pictures of explorers on the Moon. With that in mind (these traditional accounts which were nonsensical to many people of earlier times) it becomes perfectly clear that there were Gods or people with an advanced understanding and knowledge which came down from the Heavens, or space.

There are some cards with drawings on them being circulated that show Christ returning to Earth with his army of angels. They show him with a spacecraft on the right and a spacecraft on the left. Understanding this man as a human being, it seems perfectly logical that he would come back to Earth from the Heavens or space with quite a few helpers and assistants. At that point it seems perfectly natural to me that they would be traveling in some kind of vehicles; probably spacecraft.

This does not mean you should run out and approach any of the UFOs or spaceships that you happen to run into. It should also be remembered at this time that having the knowledge of advanced technology does not automatically make people good. Some who have access to advanced technology are not and unless you are able to discriminate between good and bad from a distance, it would be wise to stay out of the way.

So, to reiterate, we have one planetary overlord or angel of light out of power in a holding position here on the planet. We have the second light angel or advanced human being coming back to Earth with a space fleet in order to assume responsibility for correcting the abuses and negative conditions that have existed on Earth because of the light being who did not live up to his responsibilities. We have both planetary managers surrounded by their personnel and executives. Each group stands off the other, so we have the ingredients for a remarkable drama to be played out here on our home planet.

At this time it follows the prophecies exactly that there are many people saying: peace, peace, peace; but there is no peace. This comes from trying to enforce peace without the other prerequisites. True peace will come from expressing justice first. Peace is not an end result; it is a side effect of other actions taken.

While we have spoken of justice and peace as cause and effect, there is little doubt that the process leading up to the millennium of peace will be more chaotic than the present time. There is no escaping the fact that we have been discussing a space war involving two opposing forces off planet and on planet, simultaneously. Unfortunately the technology that we have spoken about with beneficial effects is already here, along with similar types of technology which are in all probability going to be used by the human race with disasterous effects.

Not only do we have nuclear weapons, we now have laser weapons, extremely low-frequency beam weapons, particle beam weapons, and psionic weapons. In short, we have the present technology capable of waging a Star Wars type war. While there is a high probability that this will occur, there is also a high probability, as was spoken of in the prophecies, that this period of strife and turmoil will be, and can be, cut short in order to decrease the amount of suffering people will have to endure.

The action of cutting such a period short will take

place as the forces of light gain in power and popularity upon the planet, along with these same forces going from the passive stage of talking and philosophizing, to the active stage of expressing the universal power directly in the world today.

Another significant factor involved in the end time prophecies is the statement that all of the people from other historical periods would have arisen again. I understand this to involve the spirit or soul of each person throughout history as taking up a physical body again. It could be deduced from this that with over four billion people on the planet and the population growing at a fast rate, almost everybody here has at one time or another taken part in the entire history of the Earth. There are probably very few who aren't here by now.

This is a situation that we should take into consideration as we come to the days of justice. It should also be noted that judgment, justice, and purification relate to each individual's responsibility and there is unlikely to be an opportunity to sit on the sidelines as a neutral observer or an innocent bystander in this ccritical period of our development. Therefore, it would seem a wise choice to choose your position in relation to the end time prophecies and the days of judgment and justice.

It is with this in mind that we try to make available to as many people as possible the knowledge and understanding of the present historical events unfolding in our lifetime. If anything is important at this time, it is the knowledge and ability to take a positive position in relation to the activities now taking place. Many people either consciously or intuitively understand this and are energetically seeking all the knowledge that they can possibly find about this period of time. The bottom line choice is:

A. Our traditional religions do express truth and we need to act accordingly during this time;

OR

B. Our traditional religions are fiction, so we
    need to trash them and act in an entirely
    original and creative way at this time.

What has been talked about for years will either be proved
or disproved in the near future; but either way, we will still
have to think and act.

   This shows a great deal of wisdom, along with another
inspiration for people—that of deep-seated survival instinct.
It is without a doubt one of the most interesting periods of
time in the entire history of our planet. It can be said that
the events we are experiencing have never taken place on
this large a scale or to this degree ever before. Not even
during the times of ancient civilizations such as Mu or
Atlantis, or preceding civilizations, has an experience such
as this ever reached so high a peak.

   In the following chapters, we'll take a look at future
predictability as it relates to our present-day society, and
near-future technological developments that follow in this
same area of endeavor.

PEOPLE OF CHANGE

The New Generation:
People with Personal Power

CHAPTER SEVENTEEN

VARIATIONS IN FUTURIST PREDICTIONS

"If it's smooth and slow, it's evolution. If it's fast and rough, it's change."

Most of our present-day futurist predictors see our growth as a smooth, orderly process based on past experience. The future in some cases is a continuation of the past, in other cases, it is not. Generally speaking, if it's a smooth and orderly process, it is probably decay and degeneration. If it is a rough process, with disorder, chaos, and jumps in development—as opposed to a smooth line of progression—then this disturbing process is probably growth.

In all the growth processes, there are some smooth, calm periods, but there are, by nature, quantum leaps and bounds with the introduction of variables and random elements that are very unpredictable. There have been some very unpredictable growth patterns in this century. The growth of electricity to our electrical based society was a random element that took off by itself, as was the growth of the automobile.

The growth and development of our present-day computers has taken a quantum leap in the last ten years. It has been predicted that by the year 2000, there will be home computers in 25% of the households in America. As of 1982, there are home computers in 35,000,000 homes and the growth in usage of this machine is increasing so fast that they will probably be in 25% of the homes in America by 1985, fully 15 years before predicted.

Another unpredictable random element was the burst of people seeking self-improvement and expanded consciousness with alternative learning processes that occurred in the 1960's amidst the turmoil. The generation of the 60's is one of the largest generations (the war and post-World War baby boom). These were the people who created a revolution of consciousness in the 60's. Looking into the 80's and 90's, it is difficult to predict what this large number of Americans will do during the peak productive periods of their lives.

Whatever the results, they will be different than the preceding generations. An entirely changed sense of values and way of thinking has come about in a large number of people. There has been an intense search for knowledge and understanding from this generation and the creative growth of these people has taken quantum leaps instead of a smooth progression. Anyone who thinks that the consciousness revolution of the 60's has died down is mistaken. It would be considered naive to think that was the end of it. Likewise, in our American political revolution 200 years ago, it is naive thinking to consider the revolution over. In 200 years, the American revolution has provided the foundation for the large scale revolution that is taking place during the third 100 years.

Part of this incentive is due to the fact that technological development has far outpaced social and human development. Our knowledge and information base is expanding, doubling, tripling and quadrupling every few years, while our religious, social, and political systems and governmental institutions have attempted to remain stable and unchanging.

This intense development process started with the 60's, leveled out, and is now due (in the mid-80s) to make another abrupt transition where it will bridge the gap from human to technological development, tieing the two together to form a new synthesis where the mind of man and the machines created by man are intimately interrelated, part of one system.

This will be seen in psionic and computer electronic development. The generation of today seeks to interact with their world through the world of electronics, whether it be telephones, home computers, video games, or television. In the last two decades, this interaction has been passive, with information and actions traveling one way, through an electronic based society. With the networks of computer banks, telephones, satellite and TV transmission, etc., the interaction can balance into a two-way exchange of energy and information. This means that the generation who seeks to reach out and interact in and on the world of events, can now do so from their own terminals and their own homes. At first, this seems to be a normal process and a smooth outgrowth of psionic machines (which were first invented and patented in the late 40's and early 50's); combined with computers, the process is radically changing.

This introduces a random element that is totally unpredictable. In the norm of predictability, we should have approached something very similar to the scenario presented in 1984, the book by George Orwell. However, this is not what is occurring in the realm of human development. That part is only happening in the realm of old-fashioned institutions, government, economic and religious, that resist change and growth. The influence of the integral combination of computer and psionic machines, even now, is almost unfathomable to conceive. We can foresee that individuals can reach out and interact in the active mode with the world around them, but we cannot predict exactly what individual people will do.

It is a development that will lead to very fast growth, while at the same time provide a rough sea of chaos to emerge into this world. This adds variable factors to all of the future predictions and also introduces the random element into society, civilization such as it is, that poses questions relating to our traditional prophecies.

Most prophecies have foreseen some of the chaos and have attempted to predict the outcome of this period. But now the future destiny, or unfolding of human society, is capable of changing this outcome to a significant degree.

Knowing human nature as it has developed since the consciousness and mind expansion of the last two decades, we can depend upon our brothers and sisters to take an action of some kind in order to express themselves. Because of the strong individuals incarnated here at this time, we would be hard-pressed to clearly define what these actions will affect, or how their effects will carry over into our established society.

We will have to be satisfied at present with describing the fact that this process is occurring and that we know some of the techniques and technology involved. This situation serves to stimulate creative and expanded thinking on a scale that we are not accustomed to by our education. It provides the frontier of experience directly on the cutting edge of change.

Many of the people involved are the catalysts for future developments. Engaged in this process are the pioneers and explorers of our modern times. This denotes that a new territory of experiences is being settled and developed. As with exploring any kind of new territory, we really don't know what's there until we arrive. It is in this area that human activity parallels the activity of subatomic particles with a significant amount of kinship. It also parallels the exploration of space.

Random particles are incredibly difficult to predict or measure either by speed, position, or action. This is true of individual people as well. Large groups of people and organizations can be predicted to act in a much more predictable fashion. Similarly, groups of particles such as the electrons in electricity can be predicted to follow a path along a wire and produce forecasted, exact results.

Individual particles appear at two places simultaneously and communicate with each other with no obvious direct line of communication. They travel backward in time; they jump across space/time instantaneously. They decay or transmute, growing into another type of particle. They also can split into two different particles and/or split into two particles that are of the same type.

This nebulous and uncertain process is exactly what individual people are doing. It has recently been expressed that there is a great deal of similarity between mysticism or magic and particle wave and field physics. The understanding of the Universe from these two points of view brings about many of the same observations of relationships and interrelationships in the world as we understand it.

Much of our present understanding has given us a picture of the world which is in a constant state of quick change. Like the ancient mystics, we are beginning to see the nebulous world of swirling motion and action. As our conception of the world and Universe changes, it makes me consider the younger generations of today.

I term these people "TechnoWizards", because of their mass training on video games, television, and computers. They are developing faster reflexes with quicker reaction times than many people of the preceding generations could ever imagine. This has also stimulated faster thinking processes. It's significant to remember that some members of the present generation have not just grown up with television, computers, and instantaneous transmission of pictures, thoughts, and words, but with a radically different outlook toward space development and travel. This generation considers it perfectly ordinary and routine for spaceships to be taking off and landing, as our shuttles do today. They consider it normal to have satellites, space stations and exploratory probes to the outer planets. They look forward to the space future with an attitude of excitement. We would find it difficult to predict what effect they will have during the next several decades. The only thing that can be foreseen with certainty is that they will have a dramatic effect on what's happening in our world in the near future.

It's a common saying that with growth and change in the world that it is never the same from one instant to another—one day to another. It constantly changes. It would be accurate to say that not only will the world never be the same, but it will be changing faster than ever.

The other aspect to take into account with futurist predictability is the area where we can foresee the future with a certain degree of accuracy. This is the logical outgrowth of expanded awareness in individual development over the last several decades. The one sure way to predict part of the future accurately is to consciously take part in creating that future or at least a specific area of that future. In this way, it's possible to predict the future just like predicting the building of a house. You can be reasonably sure of the outcome, although there may be a few variations, because you have designed and engineered the project.

If more and more people are sure of the parts they are creating, then we can look at the holistic view of the creation with a little more security than we do at present. As for the insecure part, a great many people are just now awakening to the fact that they have tremendous amounts of personal power. At this point they're just getting over the shock of finding this out and have not made a clear decision as to what to do with it yet, what to create. That's why the next period of time will be rough, with some chaos until people can clearly define and communicate what it is that they have decided to construct and project into their area of the Universe.

Basic trends can be assessed to some degree, one of these being that the quantum jump of individual human growth and awareness is due to have a wide ranging social, political, and economic effect on our system of society. We can foresee the outmoded and obsolete social systems attempting to maintain themselves with group survival instincts. Some of the individuals composing them will attempt to alter, reform, and change them as quickly as possible out of frustration with their ineffectiveness.

This will undoubtedly cause more economic waves (such as we are experiencing in the 80's) and even more chaotic political waves as the outmoded systems are broken down or disintegrated, with new systems being created in their place. Among the slowest to change will be some of the religious systems, followed by the governmental systems. In the free enterprise area, a matter of economic survival and a flexibility allows businesses the opportunity to adapt quickly for their own survival. You can easily discern which businesses are not adapting quickly enough to economic change and conditions. These companies eliminate themselves by their attempt to maintain obsolete methods of operating.

Many of the widest opportunities in the future will come through the business community, rather than from other institutions which are incapable of adapting. Most changes and adaptations are now affected by economic conditions in economic systems. We live in a world economic system that is very much interrelated and interdependent across all religious and political boundaries.

A good example of economic change is illustrated in our space shuttle program. Numerous companies are finding that they can research and produce products under zero gravity that cannot be produced on Earth. This includes many kinds of crystals grown for technology and many types of biological research products that can only be separated and recombined properly in an environment of zero gravity.

Probably the greatest industrial revolution which will solve many of our environmental problems on Earth will be inspired when space development is totally motivated by the free enterprise system in areas such as raw materials and mining, and then transferred directly into space stations for manufacturing. This will provide cheaper sources of raw materials and products to supply the people on Earth with the things needed for their ever-increasing standard of living.

Although slow now, in the near future, when it becomes increasingly evident that economic considerations and rules can be applied to space in a profitable manner, a quantum jump will occur in this area that will dwarf our previous industrial revolution. This will be a case where the cold world of economics will actually be creating a massive positive influx of energy and growth into the social area of human experience.

It is with positive anticipation that we look forward to this, since the space age economic development will not only cut across political and religious boundaries, but supersede government and military considerations which have proven to be counterproductive and destructive throughout our entire recorded history. This type of development and large scale trading through an economic system makes it very difficult to create wars with your neighbor. Since your neighbor happens to be a customer of yours, you generally want to remain in a good relationship so that repeated sales and trading will continue to benefit both parties. If anything in our times is revolutionary, it is the worldwide economic network which, with all its flaws and abuses, may prove more beneficial to mankind than any political or religious system that ever existed on Earth.

It should also be remembered that of all the valuable commodities and products that are traded between people, one of the most valuable, if not the most precious commodity, is new knowledge and information, or accumulated systems of information, based on experience. Knowledge and information, on an ounce by ounce level, sells for a much higher price than do minerals like gold, diamonds, and platinum.

Looking at it in this perspective, the major trading commodities of the future will be knowledge and communication of different systems that provide workable options and alternatives to the obsolete systems that we are now dealing with. In the economic social systems of the near future, knowledge is our most important product.

CHAPTER EIGHTEEN

FUTURE TECHNOLOGY DEVELOPMENT: MAGIC?

"Good News: Medical knowledge is advancing so rapidly that anyone alive after the year 2000 will be able to choose to live for as long as they want — indefinitely."

"Bad News: Past environmental abuses combined with new weapons development and the same old attitude habits of human nature make it a high probability that 90% of the 4 billion people on the Planet Earth will be dead by the year 2000!"

"Happy 21st Century to the other 10% of our population!"

Let's take a quick look at some fantastic developments, In the area of transportation, a subway train levitates magnetically at a height of two feet above the ground. This train will be able to travel coast to coast, underground, in a couple of hours. The first test model has already been built. It is a remarkable improvement in transportation.

In the developmental stage, is a computer with biological circuits enabling it to grow and expand by itself. Along with this is a computer that responds to the thoughts and emotions of the operator, without even using such advanced techniques as voice activation with machine understanding.

There is also the combination psionic/radionic machine with a modern computer that can reach out and

193

affect other people's thoughts and emotions by using a picture or plastic card with a personal code number that they carry with them. This is the foundation of planet-wide thought control.

Presently being adapted is a computer that responds to thoughts and emotions of airplane pilots, fighter pilots, and tank drivers that operate lasers. This makes reaction time much faster since there are no buttons to push.

Now let's look at the alleged Russian project that involves materializing a hand from a distance of several thousand miles away in order to steal important documents from safes and secure offices. The US military is rumored to be involved in a project that would take incoming missiles with nuclear warheads and timeshift them, projecting them back in time 50,000 years or more, so that they would explode in a different time period.

What about the report of the Navy dematerializing one of its ships at a port on the East coast and rematerializing the same ship 300 miles away during World War II?

Then there is the neutron bomb that upon explosion, removes the population without doing any damage to the property and real estate.

We could also take a look at the generators that produce extremely low frequency waves which resonate off of different electrical systems at distances of thousands of miles, affecting people's health and mental ability. We can also look at the weather modification techniques that influence weather, and as a result of that, crop and food production.

The only thing wrong with looking at these "advances in technology" in relation to the future is that they are not future developments. These are all projects that have either been built or are in some stage of development. These are all descriptions of things that are going on right now. If this is what's happening today, what in the world will future technological development bring?

Here are some other technological advances and projects that give a different look to the future.

Take another look at psionic subatomic particle technology as it applies to some more down-to-earth applications. In the area of housing and heating, there has been some research done using a combination of quartz crystal, or silicon dioxide chips, in a solution encased within the pyramid form to produce a self-sufficient house that heats itself, as well as producing its own light. This is a future development in housing with beneficial results.

In other areas there is the omnisolar electricity generator which operates by using a quartz crystal with the atomic structure of the crystals being excited in such a way as to amplify the piezoelectric effect, generating up to 23,000 volts from one small unit. This type of futuristic development is here in the early stages with some prototypes currently being tested.

On a business level, in the area of raw materials and mining, there is the psionic subatomic particle mining and mineral extractor. This machine focuses a cone-shaped field of subatomic particle beams almost a mile into the Earth to lock onto the particles of the specific mineral that is to be mined, changing its form on a subatomic structural level and extracting it directly from the Earth in a refined form. This has also been applied to the area of mineral concentrates. Instead of an elaborate separation process, the subatomic field attracts like a magnet to extract the pure form of the mineral involved. This is a futuristic development that is being tested in its prototype stage.

Particle beam research, in conjunction with purifying water and extracting the pollution particles from contaminated water sources is being done now. There are experiments for fire protection that involve extinguishing fires by using the particle beam and field generators to transmute oxygen (O) to carbon dioxide (CO_2). This is another futuristic development applied to everyday life.

There are more far-out futuristic developments. Ion Space Drives are being developed that use subatomic particle beams in order to drive space ships at near the speed of light. Crystal psi-sub devices are being experimented with as navigation units. These involve focusing the pilot's thoughts on the destination of the ship, thereby creating a line of travel. Some of these are the Star Wars generation of futuristic development; the technology of mental amplification and consciousness projection.

In medical technology, psionic subatomic particle generators are used to work through and with a human body's biomagnetic aura to clear blockages and repair short circuits in the body's electrical system adding varying degrees of energy to the affected areas. This type of technology of the future requires no chemical elements like drugs and it does not need direct physical surgery in order to perform its necessary operations.

Following closely is research with psionic subatomic particle beams which travel through cells like light speed bullets. When these particles containing their small amount of mass travel through cells in the body, they change the cell form. This can affect genetic mutations in the body, the body's offspring, and reproductive process.

Research is being done in genetics that applies to cloning and reproducing complete bodies from just one cell of another body. While this does pose a moral question, we should look at human nature again and the attitude that has abused almost every new invention, whether past, present, or future, at one time or another.

The path of progress can always be changed by human consciousness. Past experience has shown that almost all new developments or technology has been used in warlike devices first. Unless human nature changes radically in the next two decades, there will be some serious problems as a result of this bad habit.

If human development keeps pace with technology and we do change our attitude in the near future, we can expect some very beneficial results. The main one, of course, will come in the expanded life span of human beings. It would not be unreasonable to expect people in the near future to live to be the age of Methuselah—900 or 1000 years. This could be of great benefit, since it would allow people a longer lifetime to learn, understand, and develop, or it could be a nightmare. After all, if we don't grow and change our economic and political systems, we could be living in a hell on earth.

In other areas such as housing, heat, and energy usage, the benefits are unlimited. We could again develop a means of transportation which would work directly off the Earth's magnetic field. It's said of the Ancients that they sometimes transported their blocks of stone along the magnetic lines of force in the geomagnetic field. We can expect development and understanding to reach the stage of producing vehicles which levitate and ride above the ground using the Earth's own geomagnetic lines of force. These would be quietly non-polluting and energy efficient.

We can also expect the combination of the psionic machine and the computer machine to produce healthy benefits to man, enabling us to learn, grow, and understand our world and ourselves. As with the positive and negative polarities of anything we deal with, each new development can be used for benefit or harm. It would require a mass consciousness to project that a majority of the new advances in knowledge be used for beneficial purposes.

One very promising application has been described as the ultimate manufacturing machine. It would be a space-traveling machine that would extract raw materials from asteroids, moons, and planets on a subatomic particle level and run them through as purely refined metals and materials, producing the manufactured product and, at the same time, assembling them to construct all the modern conveniences, appliances, and machines that we want. It would operate in space without polluting our environment. It also would lower the cost of a very high standard of living for all of the population. This machine would control the process from beginning to end, from raw materials to manufacture. It is a radical futurist concept of technology development that has been put forth as a workable theory and may be only a little further off in our future.

Does our development of sophisticated magical technology indicate that we are developing into a new species? Who is developing a new human species? When you think of this, you automatically think of genetic research, anatomy, and drugs that increase the life span. Yet, the technology we created with the industrial revolution has affected us in a form of feedback. The water we drink, the food we eat, the air we breathe, is different than the water, food, and air of 200 or 2000 years ago.

Up to this point when we've spoken of the environmental abuses, contamination and pollution, it's been with a negative connotation, which most of it is. Some of the accumulated effects of this environmentally induced mutation have gone through a circle of feedback and actually changed the physical makeup and mental abilities of human beings. We were taught years ago that current humans are *Homo sapiens*. There are really very few *Homo sapiens* left. The affect of the different radiations and chemicals that we've created has altered the last several generations so much that a new species has developed out of them. This species is more aware of the non-material world or invisible realm than were the preceding generations. Some refer to this new species as *Homo psionus*. Because of our electricity-based technology that came about in the latter 1800's and the first part of the 1900's, everything about us has changed.

We've learned to use invisible forces in the particle realm, whether it's electrons with electricity, splitting atoms for nuclear fission, or attempting to fuse atoms together for nuclear fusion. We are dealing much more with electromagnetic radiations. Our television sets use electromagnetic radiations, as do our radios and most of the appliances in our homes. Each and everyone of these inventions create their own electromagnetic fields; the wiring in our houses create its own fields, as do our cars. Although many of these effects from these fields are beneficial, there are many that are harmful also. It would be naive to think that we have now created an electromagnetic environment and lived in it through so many generations without it having an effect on us—both our physical bodies and our mental capacities.

This is the way *Homo sapiens* evolved into the new species that is becoming dominant today: the electromagnetic species. It is very much similar to the advancements or achievements of the Atlantean scientific priesthood who learned to use the invisible energies of nature. They artificially reproduced them with higher and lower voltages as we do now.

Homo psionus takes all of the material technology in our electrically-based society and adds a dimension to it. This includes the non-physical world that exists at lower voltages, higher voltages, and neutral particles as well. *Homo psionus* is developing as people begin to understand their consciousness and its relationship to energy and matter. There is apparently no end to the possibilities of growth for the human species, except the possible end that could come about from mistakes due to ignorance and the failure to grow fast enough, or mutate and adapt fast enough, to insure advanced survival instincts in the world of today.

We are approaching the period where the ultimate technology to develop and use is ourselves. This means that we will not be responsible just for our thinking and basic material technology, but for our own genetic structure and physical makeup at the atomic and subatomic levels of matter. This can lead to an unlimited amount of positive choices to be made, or it could lead, as it has in the past, to ultimate chaos and disaster for the species itself.

The one part that does become increasingly clear again is that we must accept responsibility for the path we follow, not only as individuals, but as a species.

CHAPTER NINETEEN

QUESTIONS

*"If we've progressed so far that we have answers
for questions we haven't even thought of yet, why
don't we have answers to the questions we already
have?"*

Q: *Do we have to use only the clearest quartz crystals in
building these projects?*

A: No. Many of the Energy Rods and devices described
here have been built using chipped crystals, crystals
that were cloudy, even amethyst and smokey quartz
crystals. Although these devices worked using these
other crystals, they did not work as well as when the
clearest, most perfectly formed crystals were used.
There is a wide-open field for research in developing,
using and learning about the other types of crystals.
All the minerals we have on Earth do have their own
spectrum of radiation. There are many uses we have
barely touched on, in discovering.

Q: *Who are the experts in this field of study? Who can
we contact to learn more about this?*

A: There are practically no experts available. Most of the
researchers involved in this private study are in the
same stage of progress. The biggest achievements come
about when a group of people work together, even
starting from the beginning, and share information
with each other as they experience it.

Q: *What is an Autoelectromag?*

A: The Autoelectromag is a psionic subatomic particle gun, developed by combining the early electronic-type psionic machines of the 1940's and 50's with the advanced Atlantean technology of the Crystal Power Rods. The Autoelectromags are nicknamed the Peacemakers and Equalizers of the 1980's. In relation to the prophecies, they are spoken of as Justice Guns or Armageddon Guns. Autoelectromag is a term that covers at least three different types: the rifle, the power pistol, and the pocket pistol. These are believed to be the most powerful handheld devices ever invented by man on the planet Earth.

Q: *What is the shape of a quartz crystal?*

A: A quartz crystal is always hexagonal, six-sided. There are six sides on it and as it turns in toward the point, there will be six facets around that point. In the case of the double-termination crystal, there will be a six-sided point on each end. They come in all sizes from very tiny to some three or four feet in length.

Q: *What is the difference between a double-termination and a single-termination crystal?*

A: Again, relating to the last question, the double-termination crystal has a point on each end, with the facets intact: not two crystals growing out of the same base. The double-termination has points on opposite ends and a single-termination crystal has a point on one end only. The other end will be cloudy as it goes down to the base where it was broken off from the cluster it grew in.

Q: *Where do you buy crystals?*

A: Most rock shops have good quartz crystals in stock or can order them for you. The best crystals come from Arkansas in the U.S. and Brazil in South America.

Q: *Where can you find crystals in their natural state?*

A: Quartz crystals, the clearest ones, grow deep in the ground away from air, sunlight and water, in a limited environment. Unless you have access to underground mines in certain areas, you will probably not be able to go out and find clear quartz crystals. On the surface, in the crevices and fissures of rocks and mountains, there are numerous veins of quartz crystals. Most of these have turned cloudy from their exposure to·the elements and sunlight. Nonetheless, it is a good experience to rock hound a bit, looking for different minerals and understanding their natural areas of growth.

Q: *What about chips and cracks in crystals? Or the rainbow prism effect?*

A: Crystals that have a clear tip, even if they have a few chips and cracks, are still adequate for our uses. Occasionally, a chip will reflect and act as a prism, creating a rainbow of light down inside the crystal. These are especially sought after because of their beauty. It has not been discovered that the prism or rainbow effect enhances the activity of the crystal in our projects, since we are dealing with energies that are in a spectrum other than light.

Q: *What about storing the crystal, or insulating it in a bag?*

A: There's a great deal of debate about this. Some people store crystals in a leather bag, especially the double-termination crystals they carry with them. Other people put their crystal balls in black cloth, or black silk. You will probably find as many different opinions on how to store crystals as there are people. You should make a personal decision on how you would store or care for your crystals.

Q: *What about the serious moral questions raised by these machines?*

A: After a certain period of time, you have to answer this moral and ethical question for yourself. This takes us back to the fact that it is a personal and individual responsibility in using knowledge. There is always a certain amount of risk involved. There is always the possibility that new inventions, or new reinventions, will be used for negative or harmful purposes. This has been a part of human nature for as long as human beings have existed. In our case, the situation on Earth has reached such serious proportions that fear of doing more damage is of little consequence. If nothing at all is done right now and the situation doesn't worsen, the cumulative effects of what's happening is enough to make 90% of the life on the Earth extinct in only two decades. Many of the more harmful side-effects of our society are going to multiply, making this much more serious. Right now, anything of a positive nature is bound to be an improvement.

Q: *Don't these experiments require millions of dollars worth of equipment and operation at very high voltages?*

A: No, the materials are relatively inexpensive. The shape and type of material is of more importance than the cost. As for high voltage, the Earth, plants, animals and people all operate on low voltage electromagnetic fields. By duplicating nature, we may learn quite a bit about the use of energy, conservation, and increase our efficiency of energy usage significantly from the experience.

Q: *What about using a copper tube that's larger than ¾" or a reducer or expander coupler to change the size of the Energy Rod. What difference would this make?*

A: Numerous different sizes of rods have been built from ½ inch to 2 inches in diameter, with different sizes of crystals as well. We've found no significant increase in energy power efficiency by increasing the size of a crystal from ¾" up to 2" in size, especially in using the Rods. In the Crystal Communication Unit where a 3" diameter crystal is used, we've found this to be adequate for a large number of people. Remember, the condition and quality of the crystal is more important than its size.

Q: *What is the effect of a positive or negative attitude on* *psionic subatomic machines?*

A: The effect is tremendous since the thought particle fields actually affect or influence subatomic particles. The difference between a positive or negative attitude can make the difference between working or not working, creating a good or partial effect. A positive attitude is very necessary for advanced operation in this type of research. A negative attitude can produce a very negative effect, or can neutralize the effect all together. A positive attitude, since thoughts and emotions are the key to operation, is something to be developed.

Q: *Can this help with a person's job or to make more money?*

A: It certainly can. After a few years' experience with psionic subatomic machines, we've found that the operators develop consciousness and awareness that applies to everything from factory production to sales and almost all aspects of jobs and the economy. The awareness and experience of projecting conscious thought becomes second nature. Operators automatically start applying this to their on-the-job experience. They sometimes have remarkable successes. In some construction and manufacturing operations, one person, two, or three people at a time using these techniques in the everyday work world, have accomplished a remarkable 100% increase in productivity and efficiency. In jobs relating to sales we have seen an increase of up to 1200% in efficiency and productivity. This is a tremendous side effect. It usually takes a few years of experience before this becomes second nature. Experience pays off in productivity and an increase in finances for the operators.

Q: *Can a Healing Rod be used for a negative purpose?*

A: No. The closest to this would be when a Healing Rod dispurses or destroys a cancer or virus. As for using one for doing harm to someone else, it would be wise to note that there is a crystal in each end of the

Healing Rod. One points at the healer and one points at the subject; therefore, the feedback cycle or energy loop provides healing and good energy for the healer while it's providing the same energies for the subject involved. As you can see from this energy loop, it's in effect instant karma, and this precludes the negative or harmful uses of the Healing Rod with double crystals.

Q: *Can a Battle Rod be used for a good purpose?*

A: Yes, it can. You normally don't think of that in relation to the Atlantean Power Rod. This type of Rod can also be used for healing and to produce side effects in weather that would increase crop growth. It can be used to stimulate plant growth directly. It can be used to heal all forms of life and can be applied in dozens of different ways that are positive and healing. In this respect, there is some question as to whether the normal usage of this Rod in battle is destructive or beneficial. If there are some serious problems and contaminated areas on the Earth where the cancer of pollution consists of large groups of people doing harm, is using the Battle Rod to balance the Earth a healing operation or a destructive operation? This is a matter of definition or degree. The same applies to the Earth as it would to the human body. If you remove or destroy germs, or cut out a cancer, then this is a negative act which is creating a positive result with healing or balancing.

Q: *The perfect balance of people for operating the Crystal Communicator Unit is two male and two female. Are other groups of people okay in order to operate this?*

A: Yes, any number of people of either sex can operate this machine properly. The two and two formula is a perfect balance, but even that is not suitable unless the people operating it have balanced the male/female or positive/negative polarities within each of them. A group of people that is not balanced according to sex, but is balanced within themselves, will have the same amount of success as would four people in a two plus two polarity.

Q: *Is the disorientation, dizziness, and other side effects a thing that will pass with experience when you're using the Atlantean Crystal Headband?*

A: Usually this does pass. In fact, many people never experience the mental disorientation, dizziness or side effects, while some extremely sensitive people exhibit these effects immediately. If this does occur, take the Headband off and wait until you're settled down before you try it again. Even wait a day or so. Normally, these effects are temporary and pass quickly. If there are any side effects that continue, it's wise, like anything else, not to continue with the research using the Headband.

Q: *Can another type of pendulum, other than a quartz crystal, be used with the Pendulum Accuracy Frame?*

A: While we do recommend that the quartz crystal be used, almost any type of crystal (especially if you have a favorite one that you've been using with success for quite some time) can be adapted and mounted in the Crystal Pendulum Accuracy Frame. This frame is constructed so the crystal can be put in it or removed for outside use. If you do have a favorite pendulum that's already attuned to your frequency of energy, it may be wiser to go ahead and use it even though it's not a quartz crystal. We do feel that the quartz does lend itself to being tuned to the operator's energy field and that the quartz crystal pendulum should be used at times just to experience and see what you can do with it.

Q: *What is the maximum distance or limit of operation for these devices?*

A: There is apparently no limit except the self-induced limits of the operator. Such devices as the Crystal Communicator have been used to beam out over 400 light years in space and Energy Rods have been used within the Earth's field to reach out and effect changes at distances of over 10,000 miles. The limit or maximum distance is solely determined by the experience of the operator.

Q: *Is there any radical difference between crystal casting, or reading, and dowsing, card, or crystal ball reading?*

A: No, there isn't a radical difference. By using 12 crystals, the odds for accuracy may be improved. True skill and intuition still rest with the person doing the reading and as with any other skill, this will improve with practice.

Q: *Is there already a significant number of people in our society who carry these things around with them or use them regularly?*

A: You'd be surprised! There are quite a number of people who carry the double-termination shields. The largest number of people are those who use and carry the Atlantean Power Rods, not only here in the U.S., but also in a number of foreign countries. These implements are already becoming a regular part of our society for many people.

Q: *Are there alternatives to our future as it's predicted by the futurists or by the traditional prophecies? Or is it predetermined for us?*

A: While there are certain trends or guidelines, the alternatives to our future are varied and many, especially now that so many people are aware of their creative and powerful abilities to effect change in most areas of life. There are probably as many alternatives to our future as there are people with the power to create and effect change.

Q: *Did all of the information about these machines come from one source of hidden knowledge?*

A: No. There are many sources; most have various bits and pieces of either the description of operation or the description of the devices. All of these had to be sorted out and assimilated. There was no complete information on any of these machines readily available.

Q: *I'm attracted to the Force Knife. Should I start with that project?*

A: I wouldn't necessarily recommend that. I would recommend that you start with the Crystal Rods, Communicator, or the Headband. In exceptional cases where intuitive recall is functioning well, then a person may build the Force Knife as a first project. It would be much wiser from a common sense point of view to experience and practice with a number of the other psionic subatomic particle devices before making an attempt to construct and use the Force Knife.

Q: *Is it true that the early psionics or radionic black boxes work exactly like the sympathetic magic of the wizards, magicians and sorcerers?*

A: This is indeed the case. Early black boxes used photographs or a sample of the material in a sample plate or well and they functioned according to the laws of sympathetic magic from the ancient traditions. In fact, this was discovered when instead of using electronic parts and switches in building the early radionic boxes, cardboard representations and paper diagrams were used, spelling and drawing out the parts. These representations worked exactly like the constructed product and there was no difference in operation or efficiency. This was a remarkable discovery.

Q: *Does the fact that a person uses advanced knowledge and psionic subatomic particle machines indicate that this person is a benevolent or advanced being?*

A: No, not necessarily. There is no limit to who may obtain this type of knowledge and use it according to the laws of the Universe. Many people do develop into kind and benevolent beings because of their understanding. There is usually a small percentage who become power-crazed or negatively influenced and do not develop into benevolent beings.

Q: *Is it helpful to be knowledgeable or skilled in some of the traditional philosophies like the Native American medicine, Yoga, Sufi traditions, or Martial Arts, before using psionic subatomic particle devices?*

A: Generally, these may all help. Many of the operations and practices are similar and universal in application. There are times when an operator will pick up a Rod or one of the other devices and intuitively, instantly, be able to use it. The only explanation we can find for this would be a past lifetime; but even in this lifetime, some of these people have never studied or learned any of the skills that would be in the area of religion or esoteric knowledge. They just intuitively use them.

Q: *Is the knowledge of past lifetimes or incarnations helpful in operating these devices?*

A: There's no doubt that it can be, especially if in a previous lifetime in Atlantis or another civilization, or in incarnations closer to the present time, you had a knowledge or working experience with these devices. In this case, it would be wise to use the recalled past incarnations to reacquire a definite understanding of these as they are applied in our present day. This can be useful in readapting this type of knowledge and understanding.

Q: *Does this knowledge guarantee our survival on Earth during times of upheaval and chaos?*

A: No, but common sense indicates that more knowledge and understanding of yourself, your planet and its beings, and the universal energy that runs it all does change the odds of survival to your favor. There are no guarantees in the entire Universe except that it will all change. It's constantly changing now. There is no doubt that wider knowledge and understanding is an excellent adaptation for future survival.

Q: *Is there any one religion or philosophy that uses all of the knowledge of crystals?*

A: No, there is not. Many have bits and pieces handed down from legends, traditions, and myths. Most of the knowledge is fragmented; sometimes describing the mental attitude and characteristics necessary for it; and sometimes describing philosophies or practices that relate directly to it, the same way that many of the old religions relate to particle, field, and wave physics. There is no one religion or philosophy that deals with all of this knowledge consciously or directly.

Q: *What does a Power Rod with a double-termination crystal really do?*

A: A Power Rod with a double-termination crystal in it puts out a beam of energy in both directions, with the beam of energy at the rear turning upon itself in the chamber and reamplifying the primary beam that extends from the point of the crystal. The best comparison we can make would be the fast breeder nuclear reactor. It constantly breeds more and more energy and recreates itself instantaneously at a higher level each time. This is an extremely powerful device. It is not recommended as a project until experience with the standard Energy Rods has been developed through a great deal of practice.

Q: *Does building and using Power Rods or Staffs indicate that a person is becoming a strong warrior who will go into battle against other people?*

A: No, it does not indicate any such thing. It was pointed out earlier that the most powerful of warriors are strong enough to be gentle. The knowledge and understanding necessary in using these devices also provides alternatives for exerting a powerful positive change on the planet and its inhabitants without directly doing harm to another human being. This could be healing, teaching, and/or knowledge. It could also relate to growing crops or weather control. The point of doing battle and the position of the warrior comes from the fact that the overwhelming negative influences on the planet mean that anyone who is trying to affect a positive change probably needs the attitude and strength of a warrior to introduce it into this world, on this planet.

Q: *What types of people construct and experiment with*

these psionic machines?

A: All different kinds of people: engineers, construction workers, housewives, ironworkers, occult students, ministers, doctors, psychic healers, and psychics. People of all ages from 12 to 74 years of age have found these interesting and exciting to build and work with.

Q: *What effects will the reintroduction of Atlantean machines have on the world of today?*

A: This is very difficult to answer. We would assume that by effectively allowing more individuals to express their positive ideas, this will affect positive change in the world; however, a large scale introduction of even positive change will have a tendency to create more chaos. We would hope that by consciously taking an action in this creation that it would be planned chaos insomuch as the positive effects would be thought of ahead of the time they are introduced. This will have far-reaching effects, there is no doubt about that.

Q: *Do you really expect these devices to "change the world"?*

A: Not directly. However, there are, as we've said before, a great many people anticipating the chance to express their own ideas of change. We would expect a cumulative effect of a large number of people projecting the same positive thought forms and energy to effect changes that people think should be effected at this time.

Q: *Where do I get the silver disc to use when building the Crystal Headband?*

A: The silver disc or a solid silver coin of one ounce can be obtained from most coin shops. They are listed in the Yellow Pages under Coin Shops. As long as it's a solid silver disc, it's alright if it's a coin or ingot-type silver.

Q: *Do I have to use solid copper, or will copper-plated parts work?*

A: Due to the structure of copper itself and its relation to subatomic particles, we've found that the best effect is achieved by using solid copper. Solid copper is still very economically priced. I would recommend that solid copper be obtained instead of copper-plated parts.

Q: *Is a complete understanding of particle, wave, and field physics or mathematics necessary in order to construct and operate these machines?*

A: No, it is not. Some basic knowledge of particles may be helpful, but the Ancients had no such limitations framed within artificial constructs such as the mathematics and language of the scientific establishment of today. It is within the realm of possibility for anyone, regardless of their understanding of physics, to construct and operate these machines effectively.

Q: *As to the combination of the electronic-type psionic or radionic machine and computers, can anyone with a home computer put this combination together?*

A: Yes. Anyone can do it. It is a simple matter requiring common sense. No great knowledge of computers or psionics is necessary. This will be explained more in a later publication.

Q: *Do the recreated Atlantean artifacts require years of study, training, and practice to operate?*

A: No, not always. Some people have an instant intuitive ability to pick them up (especially the Energy Rods) and operate them. Other people require a time of experience ranging from six weeks to seven years. It depends entirely on the individual's stage of development or understanding at the present time. It usually requires far less than even a few years of experience to become accomplished.

Q: *What can I do with an Energy Rod?*

A: As quoted in the Scriptures, with the Power of God All Things are Possible. That is exactly what you are using; created within the image, you are able to project and create the effects, limited only by your mental abilities, visualization capacity, and your emotional desire to create any effects you think necessary. Many of these effects have already been covered in this book. You can do anything you can think of; of course, that usually requires understanding and persistance.

CHAPTER TWENTY

A SUMMARY OF SORTS

"If we're going to create order out of chaos, then it would be wiser to have planned chaos."

Here we are at the end of our journey. We've traveled from the cluster of Universes to our Universe; through clusters of Galaxies to our Solar System, Sun, and planets; traveled through humans, animals, plants, down to the mineral kingdom; into the crystal and subatomic structure, only to arrive at the Subatomic Age. We've traveled through time from 80,000 BC to 2050 AD, only to arrive back in the present.

At the present we've arrived in an age of chaos. It's interesting to note that even now, as the Galaxy moves into a new section of space in the Universe and is subject to new types of interstellar radiation, that chaotic conditions abound all over our planet. As the chaos increases (since it's composed of electromagnetic disturbances), psionic subatomic machines are easier to use and work more quickly through the Earth's fields, as these become more disturbed. The harder it gets for obsolete systems to operate, the easier it gets for these new systems to operate. Human nature being what it is, we probably shouldn't speculate any further on what uses this knowledge will be put to. If this book appears too brief, then again refer to the Reading List at the end of it. Each one of the listed books has dozens of references and related material. I tried to put in new information that hasn't been published before and to not duplicate anyone else's work. I've also tried to keep it short, simple, and fast-moving. I hope I've succeeded. Not only that, in spite of the serious nature of what we're talking about here, I hope everyone can relax and feel secure enough to enjoy themselves and have a good time using these new things and gaining new experiences.

DEFINITIONS

Ag Shield: As opposed to a passive protective energy force-field, this one is aggressive in that it returns the radiations sent against it back to the sender multiplied 10 to 100 times the original force.

Autoelectromag: The development of the subatomic particle power pistol by combining some of the electronic features of the early black box radionic machines with the Atlantean Power Rod. This is sometimes referred to as The Freedom Gun, The Equalizer of the 1990s, The Peacemaker, The Armageddon Gun, or The Justice Gun.

Black Box: A slang term for the electronic-type radionic and psionic machines.

Busting or Dusting: Elimination by psi-subparticle beam.

Carrier Pidgeons: Using electric lines, radio, television waves, etc. as carrier waves for psi-sub beams to reach a target.

Cats: Catalysts of change.

Double-Termination Rod or D.T. Rod: Any power Rod, Energy Rod, that uses a double-termination crystal, acting like a fast breeder reactor by feeding back in a loop, recycling itself to amplify the amount of energy involved.

Drivin' Line: A beam or beacon of subatomic thought particles being projected from quartz crystal communications devices. When these are used by the navigators of spacecraft, they are projected out to a destination light years across space; the craft then follows the line to its destination, similar to a homing device. Also used as guides for coordinating interdimensional portals.

Double-Tracking: Splitting a particle beam along a track to disable or destroy a criminal who has committed a serious destructive crime, theft, murder, etc.

Electromagnetism: Force that keeps the atoms in matter from repulsing each other, except when they have the same electrical charge; then it causes them to repulse each other.

Elf, Elves: Slang from abbreviations for very low frequency and extremely low frequency waves, used in ancient and modern warfare, both.

Fade, Fading: Projecting a psi-subparticle field far enough out to influence the minds of other persons so they don't see you in their normal vision; even though you're there, you're invisible for all practical purposes.

Fear Field: Sending out an energy field that inspires intense fear in someone's mind and emotions in order to scare them away from a direct confrontation.

(The) Fifth Force: Consciousness, referred to in ancient religions and philosophies as the key to understanding, the power within, etc. The force used by ancient priesthoods, wizards, magicians, yogis, medicine men, sorcerers, and others to control and manipulate the other four forces in order to produce what was called miracles when misunderstood by other people. In modern physics, this force was rediscovered by accident when researchers/scientists realized they, or their minds, were interfering with sub-atomic particles in their experiments.

(The) Four Forces: In Native American lore, the four winds or directions. In magic practice, the four powers. In physics, the four basic forces of gravity, weak nuclear, strong nuclear, and electromagnetism. Represented in Mu and Atlantean symbols of the crosses and swatsikas. Sometimes seen on Native American pottery, beadwork, blankets, and silverwork of today.

Force Knife: Any of the variety of knives or swords that have a psionic, subatomic particle beam generator attached or built into the handle, with a crystal on the end.

Funneling Lightspeed Particles: Using an Energy Rod or accumulator to channel particles into a beam to a certain predetermined place. This directs particles that are already in existence and already in motion. Tachyons are also manipulated in this manner.

Geo Tracking: Sending a beam of particles directly through the Earth to another point of emergence.

Geomagnetic Field Tracking: Sending a beam of particles along the lines of force in the Earth's magnetic field several feet above the ground.

Gravity: The force that acts on all matter, holding the Universe in its moving form.

Healing Rod: A Power Rod with a crystal in each end that is constructed for use in healing only.

High Field: Strong intensity beam for instantaneous results.

Homo Psionus: The new species of human beings that has developed as a result of the artificial electromagnetic radiation environment we have created for ourselves.

Hopping Out: Ancient Atlantean warriors would some-times do this when they were loosing a battle and knew they were going to die. They would leave the body con-sciously and battle their opponents from another dimen-sion, usually surprising and removing them from their body as well, technically after they, themselves, were already dead.

Human Techno Future: The future development or evo-lution of human beings and machines that far surpasses the bionic humans or the biological computers currently being developed. This involves machines such as we've been discussing where the human operator's mental patterns and emotional radiations are integrated with the operation of the machine.

Instant Karma: Eye for an eye repayment for acts committed in the present lifetime, immediately effected in this life-time.

Jumping a Wire: Instead of sending a particle beam in a straight line to its target, this technique produces the particle stream right at the target at a point in time or space without traveling a distance across space first.

Light Bullets: Not related to light as such, but to sub-atomic particles traveling at near the speed of light with mass, acting as bullets as they pass through cells in a bio-logical body.

Low Field: Weak intensity beam for slow-acting cumulative effects over a specified period of time.

Night Raiders: People traveling in their astral body at night while asleep to obtain information from normally hard-to-reach places.

P Staff or U.E.R. Staff or E.R. Staff: A longer version of the standard Power Rod.

PAF: The Pendulum Accuracy Frame; the framework for slowing down the dowsing process with a pendulum, but increasing the accuracy at the same time.

Phasing: Using psi-sub beam/field to disorient other minds at a distance.

Planned Chaos: The point in historical development where so many of the obsolete systems are breaking down and disintegrating that people consciously plan and intensify the process of breaking down old systems in order to create a space for the development and foundations of new modes of thinking and operating.

Psi-Comm: The Psionic Communicator that is used as a navigation device for spacecraft, but is now coming into popular use for projecting the consciousness of a group of people out through space in order to communicate with others in space.

Psi-Comp: The combination of a psionic black box or radionic machine with computer technology. This is one of the most significant new combinations of technologies that we have today. It also has as great a potential for evil as it does for good. This involves attaching the electronic psionic machine to a computer terminal and video screen so that the typed-in message or graphics project the desired effect programmed through the psionic computer machine.

Psi-Fi Club: Groups of people who use psionic machines for financial gain, sales, corporations, world bankers, etc; derogatory slang term.

Psi-Sub: Psionic/subatomic.

Power Rod: Any of the Atlantean Rods, Universal Energy Rods or Staffs, the longer version of the Rods, psionic/subatomic particle beam generators.

Radionics: An early name given to psionics when applied to the electronic-type black box machines invented in the 1940s or 50s.

Rainbow Shield: An extension of the white light shield under extreme intensity to the point that it separates into rays of colored light like light through a prism. This is created by very strong individuals and can extend up to ¼ mile in all directions from the one using it. In some cases, it can be expanded to almost unlimited proportions.

Sacred Fire: Subatomic particles constantly in motion interacting throughout all of creation at all times.

Scope, Scoping: Using psionic/subatomic particle machines to determine someone's exact location for a reference point.

Soul-Taker: Reference for using a psi-sub Force Knife to capture a life force instead of just disconnecting it from the body.

Storm Bringer: A warrior, changer, or person who acts as a catalyst in harmony with the Earth Mother in order to bring about strong weather conditions that disburse some of the sickness throughout the Earth, whether it be water, air, radiation-type pollution, or otherwise. The Earth itself tends to take any contaminated area or seriously ailing point and disburse it and break it up as though it were a disease. The Storm Bringer has made the conscious choice to amplify and assist the Earth as a conscious being in this process, thereby speeding up the effective cleanup of the Earth's environment.

Strong Nuclear: The bonding force of the nucleus of an atom.

Subats: Slang for psionic/subatomic particle beam machines.

Tachyons: Faster than lightspeed subatomic particles.

TechnoWizards: We've had the television generation; we now have the generation from 1960 on, in their early 20's, who have grown up with the video game-computer-TV environment and as a result are developing at a much faster rate than past generations.

Time Tracking: Sending a beam of psi-sub particles back in time to a target to create a result that was slow-acting and would manifest on the same day in the present as the time the beam was sent, even though it took six months for the reaction. A complex and touchy process.

Tracking: Shooting a particle beam along a track to disable or destroy a criminal who has committed a serious destructive crime, theft, murder, etc.

Tracks: Aura prints, biomagnetic field impressions, usually left at the scene.

U.E.R. or P-Rod: Any of the Power Rods or Universal Energy beam generators.

Unzipping: Pointing a Power Rod at the spot above a person's head and running the beam of energy down the line of chakras consecutively, usually causing unconsciousness to occur in the subject.

Visitors: Off-worlders, space people, spirits, etc.

Weak Nuclear: The force involved in nuclear decay, breaddown.

White Light Shield: A protective aura of thought particles augmenting and surrounding a person's regular biomagnetic field or Spiritual aura. This is usually used in times of danger or stress by mentally projecting and visualizing the bubble of white light. It is an esoteric practice that has been in use for thousands of years.

Wire: A path or beam of subatomic particles, derived from the electrons lining up and flowing along a copper wire when electricity is being used.

Xtal: A short abbreviation for quartz crystal, silicon dioxide crystal, SiO_2.

Double Termination Quartz Crystal: Fast Breeder type Power Rod, 1978

Left: Early Power Rod prototype with ancient crystal found near old ruins in Brazil, 1976
Right: Pendulum Accuracy Frame of hardwood and copper

Original First Model Excalibur type Force Knife, 1977

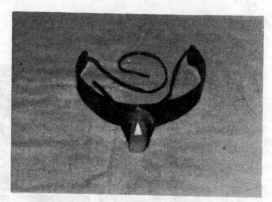

Atlantean Crystal Headband

Double Crystal Healing Rod. Large crystal has rainbow prism.

Assorted Quartz Crystals: 2 Double Termination Crystals at lower right, Pyramid and Sphere at center are optical quality

Large Quartz Crystal in solid copper Communication Unit

Rods, Force Knife and two Crystal-Tipped Staffs

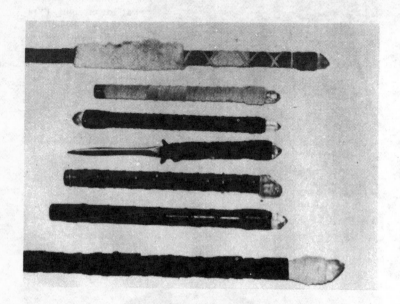

Garden Field Clusters
on white quartz rocks
around Communica-
tion Field Device

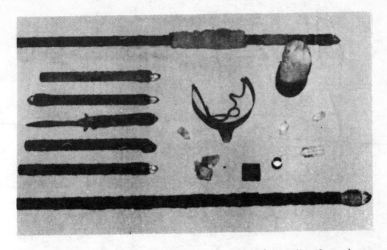

Size Relationships of various devices: Staffs (partially shown) are over 5 feet long, Crystal Ball is 1 inch in diameter

Crystal Casting Board with small quartz crystals

Four Generations of Psionic Machines: Early Radionic Box-type reproduction, Atlantean Power Rod, Autoelectromag Pistol, Pocket Pistol

Two Autoelectromags and Pocket Pistol shown with Aggressive Shield Projector

SUGGESTED READING LIST

In this book we've discussed a number of new devices, their construction and the basics of operation. In order to further understand the information in this book, I would suggest that you read some of the books in the following list. There are excellent books available that further detail certain areas we've been dealing with. The book you're now reading is meant to introduce new information and progress in this field without duplicating the earlier works of the other people involved. In combination with *Crystal Power*, the books below provide a remarkable holistic view of universal change.

From Atoms to Quarks, James S. Trefil, Copyright 1980, Charles Scribner's Sons, New York, ISBN 0-684-16484-1.

Magic: The Science of the Future, Joseph Goodavage, Copyright 1975, Signet Books, American Library, Inc., 1301 Avenue of the Americas, New York, NY 10019. *

Mysticism and the New Physics, Michael Talbot, Copyright 1981, Bantam Books, Inc., 666 Fifth Ave., New York, NY 10103, ISBN 0-553-11908-7.

New Rules, Daniel Yankelovich, Copyright 1981, Random

House, Inc., New York, ISBN 0-394-50203-5.

Other Worlds, Paul Davies, Copyright 1980, Simon & Schuster, 1230 Avenue of the Americas, New York, NY 10020, ISBN 0-671-42227-8.

Taking the Quantum Leap, Fred Alan Wolf, Copyright 1981, Harper & Row Publishers, Inc., 10 East 53rd St., New York, NY 10022, ISBN 0-06-250980-2.

The Black Box and Other Psionic Generators, W. E. Davis, Copyright 1980, T & A Publications, ContEnt, Box 156, Hancock, WI 54943.

The Collapsing Universe, Isaac Asimov, Copyright 1971, Walker & Company, New York.

The Cycles of Heaven, Guy L. Playfair & Scott Hill, Copyright 1978, Avon Books, Division of The Hearst Corporation, 959 Eighth Ave., New York, NY 10019, 77-15823 ISBN 0-380-45419-X, first Avon Printing, August 1979.

The Dancing Wu Li Masters, Gary Zukov, Copyright 1979, William Morrow and Company, Inc., 105 Madison Ave., New York, NY 10016, ISBN 0-688-03402-G.

The Tao of Physics, Fritjof Capra, Copyright 1975, Bantam Books, Bantam Books, Inc., 666 Fifth Ave., New York, NY 10019, ISBN 0-553-14306-2.

The Awesome Force, Joseph B. Cater, Cadake Industries, P.O. Box 9478, Winterhaven, Florida, 33880.

* of special interest

STAYING IN TOUCH

On the following pages you will find listed, with their current prices, some of the books and tapes now available on related subjects. Your book dealer stocks most of these, and will stock new titles in the Llewellyn series as they become available. We urge your patronage.

However, to obtain our full catalog, to keep informed of new titles as they are released and to benefit from informative articles and helpful news, you are invited to write for our bi-monthly news magazine/catalog. A sample copy is free, and it will continue coming to you at no cost as long as you are an active mail customer. Or you may keep it coming for for a full year with a donation of just $5.00 in U.S.A. ($7.00 for Canada & Mexico, $10.00 overseas, first class mail). Many bookstores also have *The Llewellyn New Times* available to their customers. Ask for it.

Stay in touch! In *The Llewellyn New Times'* pages you will find news and reviews of new books, tapes and services, announcements of meetings and seminars, articles helpful to our readers, news of authors, advertising of products and services, special money-making opportunities, and much more.

The Llewellyn New Times
P.O. Box 64383-Dept. 725, St. Paul, MN 55164-0383, U.S.A.

★　　　★　　　★

TO ORDER BOOKS AND TAPES

If your book dealer does not have the books and tapes described on the following pages readily available, you may order them direct from the publisher by sending full price in U.S. funds, plus $1.00 for handling and 50¢ each for postage within the United States; outside USA surface mail add $1.00 per item. Outside USA air mail add $7.00 per item.

FOR GROUP STUDY AND PURCHASE

Because there is a great deal of interest in group discussion and study of the subject matter of this book, we feel that we should encourage the adoption and use of this particular book by such groups by offering a special "quantity" price to group leaders or "agents".

Our Special Quality Price for a minimum order of five copies of CRYSTAL POWER is $29.85 Cash-With-Order. This price includes postage and handling within the United States. Minnesota residents must add sales tax. For additional quantities, please order in multiples of five. For Canadian and foreign orders, add postage and handling charges as above. Credit Card (VISA, MasterCard, American Express, Diners' Club) Orders are accepted. Charge Card Orders only may be phoned free within the U.S.A. by dialing 1-800-THE MOON. Customer Service calls dial 1-612-291-1970 and ask for "Kae". Mail Orders to:

LLEWELLYN PUBLICATIONS
P.O. Box 64383-Dept. 725 / St. Paul, MN 55164-0383, U.S.A.

About the Author

Michael Smith is an inventor and author who has worked for over a decade to recreate the crystal artifacts of ancient civilizations for individual development in our present day society. This has created a new synthesis of ancient crystal Supertechnology with our modern high technology in the areas of health, communications, plant growth, energy, and frontier research for a positive future. He has provided lectures, workshops, and seminars on the crystal relationship to balanced human development in the Northwest. His articles and publications have been used by private researchers across the United States and in eight foreign countries as reference works for the developing crystal technology. His inventions range from the crystal energy rods and headbands of Atlantis to crystal energy beam/field projectors, including the first crystal interface for using home computers with psionic black box-type machines. His style of writing has produced information so easy to read and understand that it's been referred to as the first popular mechanics guide to the paranormal. He spent some years with a Native American Medicine Man to learn the knowledge of traditional Americans. It was during this time that he discovered the ancient knowledge of quartz crystals and its relationship to today's subatomic particle physics. He is presently living in Colorado, working for a high tech electronics company while engaged in crystal research and writing. He is corresponding with people who are working to establish an International Crystal Information Network. His main goal is to unite science, religion, politics, and business with the motivation of the One Creative Universal Force in order to solve our problems of energy, pollution, poverty, and the threat of nuclear war while at the same time, increasing individual development and our standard of living.

Anyone wishing to correspond with Michael can write to him at this address:

Michael G. Smith
P.O. Box 26881
Lakewood, CO 80226

THE LLEWELLYN PRACTICAL GUIDES
by Melita Denning & Osborne Phillips

THE LLEWELLYN PRACTICAL GUIDE TO ASTRAL PROJECTION.
Yes, your consciousness can be sent forth, out-of-the-body, with full awareness and return with full memory. You can travel through time and space, converse with non-physical entities, obtain knowledge by non-material means, and experience higher dimensions.

> Is there life-after-death? Are we forever shackled by Time & Space? The ability to go forth by means of the Astral Body, or Body of Light, gives the personal assurance of consciousness (and life) beyond the limitations of the physical body. No other answer to these ageless questions is as meaningful as experienced reality.

The reader is led through the essential stages for the inner growth and development that will culminate in fully conscious projection and return. Not only are the requisite practices set forth in step-by-step procedures, augmented with photographs and puts-you-in-the-picture" visualization aids, but the vital reasons for undertaking them are clearly explained. Beyond this, the great benefits from the various practices themselves are demonstrated in renewed physical and emotional health, mental discipline, spiritual attainment, and the development of extra faculties".

Guidance is also given to the Astral World itself: what to expect, what can be done—including the ecstatic experience of Astral Sex between two people who project together into this higher world where true union is consumated free of the barriers of physical bodies.

0-87542-181-4, 239 pages, 5¼ x 8, softcover   **$7.95**

SUPPLEMENTAL DEEP MIND TAPE

THE LLEWELLYN DEEP MIND TAPE FOR ASTRAL PROJECTION.
This is a tool so powerful that it is offered only for use in conjunction with the above book. The authors of this book are adepts fully experienced in all levels of psychic development and training, and have designed this 90-minute cassette tape to guide the student through full relaxation and all the preparations for projection, and then—with the added dimension of the authors personally produced electronic synthesizer patterns of sound and music—they program the Deep Mind through the stages of awakening, and projection of, the astral Body of Light. And then the programming guides your safe return to normal consciousness with memory—enabling you to bridge the worlds of Body, Mind and Spirit.

> The Deep Mind Tape is a powerful new technique combining guided Mind Programming with specially created sound and music to evoke deep level response in the psyche and its psychic centres for controlled development, and induction of the OUT-OF-BODY EXPERIENCE.

3-87542-201, 90-minute cassette tape.   **$9.95**

Note: If you have the book, THE LLEWELLYN PRACTICAL GUIDE TO ASTRAL PROJECTION, you may order this DEEP MIND TAPE by sending full price, plus $1.50 postage & handling ($7.00 overseas airmail). Or, you can order both Book AND Tape for a special price of just $15.00 Postpaid in U.S.A. ($25.00 overseas airmail).

THE LLEWELLYN PRACTICAL GUIDE TO CREATIVE VISUALIZATION. All things you will ever want must have their start in your mind. The average person uses very little of the full creative power that is his, potentially. It's like the power locked in the atom—it's all there, but you have to learn to release it and apply it constructively.

> **IF YOU CAN SEE IT ... in your Mind's Eye ... you will have it! It's true: you can have whatever you want—but there are "laws" to Mental Creation that must be followed. The power of the mind is not limited to, nor limited by, the Material World—Creative Visualization enables Man to reach beyond, into the Invisible World of Astral and Spiritual Forces.**

Some people apply this innate power without actually knowing what they are doing, and achieve great success and happiness; most people, however, use this same power, again unknowingly, INCORRECTLY, and experience bad luck, failure, or at best unfulfilled life.

This book changes that. Through an easy series of step-by-step, progressive exercises, your mind is applied to bring desire into realization! Wealth, Power, Success, Happiness ... even Psychic Powers ... even what we call Magickal Power and Spiritual Attainment ... all can be yours. You can easily develop this completely natural power, and correctly apply it, for your immediate and practical benefit. Illustrated with unique, "puts-you-into-the-picture" visualization aids.

0-87542-183-0, 255 pages, 5¼ x 8, softcover.   **$7.95**

THE LLEWELLYN PRACTICAL GUIDE TO THE MAGICK OF THE TAROT. *How to Read, And Shape, Your Future.*

"To gain understanding, *and control*, of Your Life."—Can anything be more important? To gain insight into the circumstances of your life—the inner causes, the karmic needs, the hidden factors at work—and then to have the power to change your life in order to fulfill your real desires and True Will: that's what the techniques taught in this book can do.

Discover the Shadows cast ahead by Coming Events.

Yes, this is possible, because it is your DEEP MIND—that part of your psyche, normally beyond your conscious awareness, which is in touch with the World Soul and with your own Higher (and Divine) Self—that perceives the *astral shadows* of coming events and can communicate them to you through the symbols and images of the ancient and mysterious Tarot Cards.

> **Your Deep Mind has the power to shape those astral shadows—images that are causal to material events—when you learn to communicate your own desires and goals using the Tarot's powerful symbol language and the meditative and/or ritual techniques taught in this book to energize and imprint new patterns in the Astral Light.**

This book teaches you both how to read the Tarot Cards: seeing the likely outcome of the present trends and the hidden forces now at work shaping tomorrow's circumstances, and then—as never before presented to the public—how you can expand this same system to bring these causal forces under your conscious control.

> The MAGICK of the Tarot mobilizes the powerful inner resources of psyche and soul (the source of all Magick, all seemingly miraculous powers) by means of meditation, ritual, drama, dance for the attainment of your goals, including your spiritual growth.

0-87542-198-9, 252 pages, 5¼ x 8, illust., softcover.   **$7.95**

PRACTICAL CANDLEBURNING RITUALS
by Raymond Buckland, Ph. D.

Another book in Llewellyn's Practical Magick series. Magick is a way in which to apply the full range of your hidden psychic powers to the problems we all face in daily life. We know that normally we use only 5% of our total powers—Magick taps powers from deep inside our psyche where we are in contact with the Universe's limitless resources.

Magick need not be complex—it can be as simple as using a few candles to focus your mind, a simple ritual to give direction to your desire, a few words to give expression to your wish.

This book shows you how easy it can be. Here is Magick for fun, Magick as a Craft, Magick for Success, Love, Luck, Money, Marriage, Healing; Magick to stop slander, to learn truth, to heal an unhappy marriage, to overcome a bad habit, to break up a love affair, etc.

Magick—with nothing fancier than ordinary candles, and the 28 rituals in this book (given in both Christian and Old Religion versions)—can transform your life. Illustrated.

ISBN: 0-87542-048-06, 189 pg., 5¼ x 8, softbound.   **$5.95**

EARTH POWER
by Scott Cunningham

This is a book of folk magic—the magic of the common people. As such, it is different from nearly every other published work on the subject. This book is for the people of the Earth. The practices are as easy as placing a leaf in a north wind. The ritual is married to the forces of Nature. This is natural magic rediscovered. This book can not only help you learn these natural magical methods, but it can also put you in touch with the planet that nurtures you.

ISBN: 0-87542-121-0, 5¼ x 8, illustrated, softbound.   **$6.95**

COLOR MAGIC by Raymond Buckland

The world is a rainbow of color, a symphony of vibration. We have left the Newtonian idea of the world as being made of large mechanical units, and now know it as a strange chaos of vibrations ordered by our senses, but, our senses are limited and designed by Nature to give us access to only those vibratory emanations we need for survival.

But, we live far from the natural world now. And the colors which filled our habitats when we were natural creatures have given way to grey and black and synthetic colors of limited wave lengths determined not by our physiological needs but by economic constraints.

Raymond Buckland, author of the world-famous PRACTICAL CANDLE BURNING RITUALS has produced a fascinating and useful new book, PRACTICAL GUIDE FOR COLOR MAGIC which shows you how to reintroduce color into your life to benefit your physical, mental and spiritual well-being!

- Learn the secret meanings of color.
- Use color to change the energy centers of your body.
- Heal yourself and others through light radiation.
- Discover the hidden aspects of your personality through color.

PRACTICAL COLOR MAGIC will teach all the powers of light and more! You'll learn new forms of expression of your inner-most self, new ways of relating to others with the secret languages of light and color. Put true color back into your life with the rich spectrum of ideas and practical magical formulas form COLOR MAGIC!

ISBN: 0-87542-047-8, 200 pp., illustrated   **$5.95**

MAGICAL STATES OF CONSICOUSNESS
by Melita Denning and Osborne Phillips

Magical States of Consciousness are dimensions of the Human Psyche giving us access to the knowledge and powers of the Great Archetypes that pertain to all existence.

These dimensions are attained as we travel the Paths of the Qabalah's Tree of Life—that "blueprint" to the structure of the Lesser Universe of the Human Psyche and to the Greater Universe in which we have our being.

Published here for the first time are not only the complete texts for these inward journeys to the Deep Unconscious Mind, but complete guidance to their application in Spiritual Growth and Initiation, Psychological Integration and "Soul Sculpture" (the secret technique by which we may shape our own character).

Here, too, are *Magical Mandalas* for each of the Path-Workings that serve as "doorways" to altered states of consciousness when used with the Path-Working narrations, and *Magical Images* of the Sephirothic Archetypes as used in invoking those powerful forces.

It's all here in these newly revealed techniques of the Western Esoteric Tradition.

0-87542-194-6, 420 pages, Illust.,soft. $12.95

MAGICAL RITES FROM THE CRYSTAL WELL
by Ed Fitch

In nature, and in the Earth, we look and find beauty. Within ourselves we find a well from which we may draw truth and knowledge. And when we draw from this well, we rediscover that we are all children of the Earth.

The simple rites in this book are presented to you as a means of finding your own way back to nature; for discovering and experiencing the beauty and the magic of unity with the source.

These are the celebrations of the seasons: at the same time they are rites by which we attune ourselves to the flow of the force—the energy of life. These are rites of passage by which we celebrate the major transitions we all experience in life.

Here are the Old Ways, but they are also the Ways for Today.

0-87542-230-6, 147 pages, 7 x 10, illust. $13.00

LLEWELLYN'S QUARTZ CRYSTALS

Beautiful natural quartz crystals to use in the devices described in *Crystal Power*. Llewellyn now has a good supply of crystals that were mined in Arkansas. They come in two sizes and are high energy crystals. They are all single terminated and are clear at the point. We look them over before we send them to you so you are guaranteed of getting one of the finest crystals available. With one of our crystals and this book, you will be able to construct a powerful tool.

Crystal A, approx. 2 inches long, $ 7.00 + $1.00 postage
Crystal B, approx. 3½ inches long, $17.00 + $1.50 postage

LLEWELLYN'S GEMSTONES

Healers and magicians have always used special stones in their work. We are now offering some of these special stones, each endowed by legend and ancient tradition with specific powers.

GEM•PACK I contains one each of the following four stones: Amethyst (to aid in spiritual cleansing, dreamwork), Bloodstone (stop bleeding), Carnelian (healing and calming fears), and Tiger Eye (protection).

GEM•PACK II contains one each of the following four stones: Rose Quartz (love), Lace Agate (vitality), Sodalite (raise spiritual emotions), and Apache Tear Drop (said to be the frozen tears of Apache women weeping over their dead).

GEM•PACK I **$5.00**
GEM•PACK II **$5.00**